EVERYTHING ROCK 'N' ROLL FANS SHOULD KNOW

FANS SHOULD KNOW

Explore the 1950s Beginnings, 1960s British Invasion, 1970s Hard Rock, 1980s Metal Mayhem, 1990s Alternative, and More!

COLIN PIKE

ISBN: 978-1-962496-17-9

For questions, please reach out to
Support@OakHarborPress.com

Please consider leaving a review!

Just visit: OakHarborPress.com/Reviews

FREE BONUS

SCAN ME!

GET OUR NEXT BOOK FOR FREE!
Scan or go to:
OakHarborPress.com/Free

TABLE OF CONTENTS

INTRODUCTION

Rock 'n' roll originated in 1950s America during a time of social and cultural change. This new genre of music blended the traditionally–African American and Black sounds of blues and gospel with the traditionally-White sounds of country and swing music. Rock music took root in youth culture as it gained popularity on the radio, with record companies, and eventually on television. Young people associated rock with freedom and rebellion and embraced the genre as a way to reject the traditions and expectations of older generations.

Rock 'n' roll evolved to become a source of commonality among a wide variety of racial, social, economic, and cultural groups, inspiring and connecting both musicians and fans across the world. This led to the genre's association with counterculture and the push for freedom and social reform, especially in the 1960s.

Since then, many subgenres and innovations have shaped rock 'n' roll—from punk to grunge, legendary arena performances to iPhones—yet the power of rock music primarily lies in its ability to challenge convention and push traditional boundaries. Rock 'n' roll is a symbol of both rebellion and unification, as well as a unique and important form of artistic expression and human interaction.

PART ONE:
THE BIRTH OF ROCK 'N' ROLL
(1950s)

1950

When people think of 1950s America, images of nuclear families living in picket-fenced suburbia probably come to mind. This decade reflected many aspects of American progress and prosperity, post–World War II. There were "booms" in technology, the economy, industry, and babies, in addition to a conservative political and societal push for stability, conformity, and "traditional" values. Yet many counterculture movements took root in this decade, including civil rights, free political speech, and the beatnik subculture.

Consequently, the support of young Americans in the 1950s led to the birth of rock 'n' roll as they wished to rebel against their parents, musically and otherwise. During this decade, young people gained unprecedented access to music through radio, records, and television. In addition, rock 'n' roll appealed to kids from diverse racial, economic, and sociocultural backgrounds. To the baby boomers, this popular music and its artists symbolized freedom, collective rebellion, love, and an appealing sound that older generations found to be somewhere between distasteful and downright dangerous.

[1]
THE ROOTS OF ROCK 'N' ROLL

Some might say that rock 'n' roll has roots in nearly all previous musical forms because of its many influences and the gradual evolution of the genre. Certainly, much of today's rock music stems from rhythm and blues (R&B), electric blues, gospel, jazz, folk, country music, and more. Pop music of the early 1950s, the precursor to the beginnings of rock music in the mid- to late-1950s, grew out of the big band and swing music from the 1930s and '40s. Western swing upped the tempo of country music during this time, as well.

However, it was the R&B music of Black Americans in the late 1940s and early 1950s that formed the strongest roots of rock music. White artists began to cover R&B songs, which led to a wider audience and spots on pop music charts. This crossover — what many would consider overt cultural appropriation today — eventually made way for Black artists' original recordings to be heard, which, in turn, promoted the popularity of rock 'n' roll as a new genre created by artists of both races.

Perhaps the best example of this phenomenon is the career and contribution of Alan Freed, a radio DJ in Cleveland, Ohio. His "Moondog Show" offered hits from R&B, country, jazz, jump blues, and boogie artists. Freed's goal was to introduce this "crosscurrent" of genre and style to an audience of teenagers — both Black and White. Freed labeled the music rock 'n' roll, helping to produce and promote the new genre across America and, eventually, the globe. This not only expanded 1950s pop culture but also helped break down racial barriers, as teenagers of all races shared cultural touchstones through listening to the same music.

[2]
ELVIS PRESLEY:
THE KING OF ROCK 'N' ROLL

Elvis Presley was born in January 1935 in Tupelo, Mississippi. Not only did he become the "King of Rock 'n' roll," but he remains one of the most important musical and cultural performers of the 20th century.

Elvis's career began in Memphis, with Sam Phillips at Sun Records in 1954, when he was just a teenager. A year later, Colonel Tom Parker became his manager, and Elvis's "Heartbreak Hotel" became a number-one single. His songs and performance style on television initially caused many Americans to believe that Elvis would morally corrupt young listeners.

However, his music career achieved unprecedented success and even led to an acting career in Hollywood.

In 1958, Elvis was drafted into the military. Two years later, and for much of the 1960s, he made commercially-successful films and soundtrack albums. In 1968, Elvis appeared in a landmark "comeback" special televised by NBC. This led to a concert residency in Las Vegas and other tours as well. In 1973, Elvis once again made history with *Aloha from Hawaii*, the first solo concert to be broadcast globally.

Unfortunately, due to his lifestyle and prescription drug abuse, Elvis's health deteriorated, leading to his death in August 1977 in his Graceland home.

It's nearly impossible to quantify the influence Elvis Presley had on rock music and pop culture. Across the world, people still recognize hits like "Jailhouse Rock," "Viva Las Vegas," "Suspicious Minds," "Hound Dog," "Burning Love," and "Blue Suede Shoes" today.

Elvis pioneered the image of a rock star and even achieved commercial success in other genres, such as country, rockabilly, R&B, and gospel. One of the bestselling, most well-known, and revered artists of all time, Elvis, won three Grammys over the course of his career, receiving the Grammy Lifetime Achievement Award at just 36 years old. His solo career charts and archetypal performances are unmatched, and many historians credit Elvis with revolutionizing the world of music.

The Rock & Roll Hall of Fame inducted Elvis Presley in 1986, and he received the Presidential Medal of Freedom in 2018. It's fair to say Elvis's legacy will last as long as music itself.

[3]
CHUCK BERRY:
THE GUITAR PIONEER

Charles Edward Anderson Berry, commonly known as Chuck Berry, was born in St. Louis, Missouri, in October 1926. His mother was among the first Black women of her generation to receive a college education, while Berry's father was a carpenter and deacon in the Baptist church.

Chuck Berry grew up in a segregated Black community but was exposed to music in both school and church. He taught himself to play guitar, combining blues and country to achieve new sounds. In 1955, Berry was signed by Chess Records and released his first hit, "Maybellene," considered by some to be the first legitimate rock 'n' roll song. He continued with influential singles such as "Roll Over Beethoven," "Johnny B. Goode," "Nadine," and "No Particular Place to Go."

Most musicians and historians consider Chuck Berry to be the father of rock 'n' roll, not only defining the genre but also shaping its trajectory. This is especially evident in the way Berry pioneered the guitar as the main instrument in the genre. Not only did Berry put the guitar at the forefront of rock music, but he revolutionized the way it was played through improvised moves on stage that captivated audiences and inspired future rock guitarists.

Berry was the first inductee of the Rock & Roll Hall of Fame in 1986 and won the Grammy Lifetime Achievement Award in 1985. His music appeared on R&B and pop charts and crossed racial lines, capturing common themes that resonated with young listeners, both Black and White.

However, Chuck Berry's personal life had an unfortunate impact on his music career, especially with his 1959 conviction under the Mann Act for transporting an underage girl across state lines.

Though he was released from prison in 1963, Berry never regained the level of success he'd enjoyed prior to his incarceration. Nevertheless, there's no debating his legendary talent as a musician, songwriter, and performer.

Berry's legacy is marked by the fact that his recording of "Johnny B. Goode" is the only rock song to be included on the spacecraft *Voyager* when it was launched in 1977.

[4]
LITTLE RICHARD: THE WILD ONE

Little Richard was born Richard Wayne Penniman in 1932 in Macon, Georgia. He grew up singing gospel in his church choir, where he learned to play the piano as well. Unfortunately, Richard's father forced him out of their home as a young teenager after learning of his homosexuality. Richard became a vocalist for traveling groups performing in Black music venues. His youth earned him the iconic name "Little Richard." While touring, he was influenced by gospel and R&B, and in 1951, he won a contest that led to a contract with RCA Records.

However, it wasn't until 1955 that Richard recorded a demo of "Tutti Frutti" and sent it to Specialty Records in Los Angeles. The song was one of the first to appear on both the R&B and pop charts, making Little Richard one of the first Black musicians to enjoy commercial success with White audiences.

"Tutti Frutti" was followed by such hits as "Long Tall Sally," "Good Golly Miss Molly," and "Lucille." In 1957, Little Richard exited the rock 'n' roll scene to become a minister and gospel singer. Then, in 1964, the Beatles recorded "Long Tall Sally," prompting Little Richard to revive his career. He recorded music, released albums, and performed all over the world, even appearing on *Sesame Street* in 1994 to sing a rendition of "Rubber Duckie" in his own unique style.

Little Richard will be remembered for his wild performances and big personality, as well as his advocacy for Black performers. He was inducted into the Rock & Roll Hall of Fame in 1986 and won several prestigious awards before his death in 2020. Jimi Hendrix, the Beatles, and David Bowie all credit Little Richard as an inspiration, and his music continues to influence musicians today.

[5]
BUDDY HOLLY & THE CRICKETS: EARLY INNOVATORS

Charles Hardin Holley, later known as Buddy Holly, was born in Lubbock, Texas, in 1936. Today, his pioneering influence on rock music in the 1950s is still felt.

Buddy Holly performed as a country-western musician until 1955 when he and his band—then known as Buddy and Bob—opened for Elvis Presley and Bill Haley & His Comets. From then on, he focused on rock music as a singer/songwriter.

In early 1957, Buddy Holly formed a band called the Crickets, which released their hit song, "That'll Be the Day," later that year. Band members included Buddy Holly on vocals and guitar, Niki Sullivan on guitar, Jerry Allison on drums, and Joe B. Mauldin on bass.

Buddy Holly & the Crickets were early innovators of rock 'n' roll with their blend of original material and a performance setup of two guitars, bass, and drums. They influenced several future rock groups, including the Beatles, who some historians believe chose their band name in part as a tribute to Buddy Holly & the Crickets. The band went on to write and record a slew of hits, including "Everyday," "Peggy Sue," "Maybe Baby," and "It's So Easy!"

Tragically, on February 3, 1959, Buddy Holly was killed in a plane crash near Clear Lake, Iowa. His death at age 22, in addition to that of Ritchie Valens and J.P. Richardson Jr., known as "The Big Bopper," inspired Don McLean's song "American Pie." The 1971 elegy to the three rock idols names the plane crash as the "day the music died."

In 1986, Buddy Holly was inducted posthumously into the Rock & Roll Hall of Fame. He's remembered for popularizing rock as a genre with his unique sound and sophisticated songwriting. Buddy Holly was also among the first rock musicians to use experimental recording effects such as double tracking to establish layers and depth of sound.

[6]
JERRY LEE LEWIS: THE PIANO MASTER

Jerry Lee Lewis was born in 1935 in Ferriday, Louisiana. Though his family was poor, his father recognized Jerry Lee's love and skill for the piano and mortgaged their home to purchase one.

Lewis was heavily influenced by Black R&B musicians and southern preachers, along with Elvis Presley, which led him to Memphis, Tennessee, and Sun Records. Thus began his rise to stardom, with hits such as "Whole Lotta Shakin' Goin' On" and "Great Balls of Fire" in the late 1950s.

Lewis was a contemporary of Elvis, Little Richard, and Chuck Berry, yet he had a performance style all his own. He was a master piano player but would also play the keys with his elbow or heel on stage. Audiences gravitated as much toward his showmanship as his music.

Unfortunately, Lewis faced personal crises such as addiction and inner conflict between his religious upbringing and rock 'n' roll lifestyle. In addition, he faced a scandal in 1958 — and subsequent boycott of his music — when the public learned of his marriage to his 13-year-old cousin.

Despite many setbacks, Jerry Lee Lewis, nicknamed the "Killer," continued to record music and perform throughout the decades. He's remembered not only as a master of the keys but a pioneer of rock 'n' roll performance and music legend. Though Lewis turned to country music in the late 1960s, he was inducted into the Rock & Roll Hall of Fame in 1986.

[7]
THE IMPACT OF SUN RECORDS

Sun Records was established in 1952 when Sam Phillips rented a small storefront on Union Avenue in Memphis, Tennessee. The store is considered key to the birth of rock 'n' roll, as it provided a space for musicians to record their songs.

Though Phillips grew up listening to various musical styles in Alabama, it was a trip to Memphis in 1939 and the captivating music of Beale Street that led him to open his recording studio there. His goal was to give Black artists a platform to record blues music; to that end, Phillips set up equipment so customers could pay to record something and take it with them.

Until the mid-1950s, Sun Records primarily served as a place for Black artists such as B.B. King and Howlin' Wolf to record their music. Phillips encouraged artists to develop their own authentic sound, even if it was a bit rough. This allowed for a blend of musical styles that not only shaped R&B as a genre but also helped the rock 'n' roll genre cross racial lines and become part of the mainstream music scene. Yet, due to the climate of racism and segregation — especially in the south — Phillips recognized the narrow audience for R&B among White people.

One day, Elvis Presley walked into Sun Records and changed music history. Within a year, Phillips had released five of Elvis's singles and sold his contract to RCA for $35,000—the highest price for any pop artist at the time. From 1956 to 1957, Carl Perkins, Johnny Cash, Roy Orbison, and Jerry Lee Lewis all recorded hits with Sun Records.

Sam Phillips was inducted into the Rock & Roll Hall of Fame in 1986 for his contribution to the music world through its legendary artists and pioneering independent label, along with the way Phillips embraced individuality, diversity, and originality in the industry.

[8]
ICONIC PERFORMANCE: ELVIS ON *THE ED SULLIVAN SHOW*

There's no shortage of memorable rock 'n' roll performances, but perhaps the most iconic is Elvis Presley's first appearance on *The Ed Sullivan Show*. Elvis was known for having performed on other television shows, having already released his first hit album. However, on September 9, 1956, over 60 million viewers tuned in to watch as Elvis made music and television history.

Elvis's performance reflected the clash of cultures in America at the time. At first, even Ed Sullivan had resisted booking him, fearing criticism by conservative adults over Presley's "inappropriate" movements and gestures.

However, over 80 percent of American viewers watched the singer's musical debut on Sullivan's show, making it the equivalent of a nationwide event and a cultural touchstone for people in the music and entertainment industries.

Elvis performed "Don't Be Cruel," "Love Me Tender," and part of "Hound Dog" on the show with great success. Interestingly, Elvis's performance on *Ed Sullivan* was not broadcast live because he was on location in Hollywood for the movie *Love Me Tender*. Instead, he was filmed on a soundstage in Los Angeles.

Ironically, Ed Sullivan was not in the theater to host that program, either. Sullivan was recovering in the hospital from serious injuries as a result of a nearly fatal car crash, so British actor Charles Laughton filled in as host.

Elvis Presley appeared on *The Ed Sullivan Show* two more times, and Sullivan assured his audience — on camera — that Elvis was a "real decent, fine boy" and "a very nice person."

Elvis Presley's music and style embodied rock 'n' roll and youth culture in 1950s America, and his iconic performance on *The Ed Sullivan Show* marked a turning point in his career — and an important moment in the birth of rock 'n' roll.

[9]
LANDMARK ALBUM:
CHUCK BERRY'S *BERRY IS ON TOP*

Berry Is on Top was Chuck Berry's top-selling third album, released in 1959. Recorded at Chess Studio in Chicago and produced by Leonard and Phil Chess, *Chuck Berry Is on Top* includes several of his most well-known songs, including "Maybellene," "Johnny B. Goode," and "Roll Over Beethoven." Six of the twelve album tracks were released as singles, many of which are considered classics to this day with their pop hooks. All songs are credited to Berry, who paved the way for singer-songwriters' ownership of their music.

Many musicians and rock 'n' roll enthusiasts consider *Chuck Berry Is on Top* as the first defining rock album and a landmark in the genre's format. Bands such as the Rolling Stones, the Beatles, the Doors, and musicians from David Bowie to Jimi Hendrix have covered songs from this revolutionary album. *Chuck Berry Is on Top* is also considered a key element in fueling the British

Invasion of the 1960s, particularly Berry's lead-guitar playing style. Chuck Berry's combination of jazz rhythm and unique guitar solos represented a modern sound, making the album an invaluable compilation of hit songs that are still influential and appreciated today.

[10]
ROCK 'N' ROLL'S FIRST HIT: BILL HALEY'S "ROCK AROUND THE CLOCK"

Not only is "Rock Around the Clock" considered the first hit in the rock 'n' roll genre, but at one time, it was estimated to be playing somewhere across the globe every minute of the day. The original song was written by Max C. Freedman and James E. Myers in 1952, with the title "We're Gonna Rock Around the Clock Tonight!" Though Bill Haley & His Comets was not the first band to record the song, Haley's 1954 version with Decca Records is the most well-known. It was also the first rock 'n' roll record to top the charts in both the US and UK.

Bill Haley's recording came to represent youthful rebellion in the 1950s when it was included in the soundtrack of the movie *Blackboard Jungle* in 1955. As legend has it, when the movie's producers were looking for a song, one of the principal actors, Glenn Ford, borrowed some records from his son. "Rock Around the Clock" by Bill Haley & His Comets was a B-side among those records and was chosen by the producers to be featured in the movie. When the single was re-released, it was the first rock 'n' roll song to hit number one on the Billboard pop chart, spreading like wildfire across the world.

Anyone old enough to have seen the first two seasons of *Happy Days* will remember the image of a spinning record and "Rock Around the Clock" playing as the opening theme song, which Haley had re-recorded for the show. This was just months after the original version appeared in the movie *American Graffiti,* which put it back on the charts in 1974.

Haley's recording is considered among the greatest songs of all time, and it is the single that introduced rock 'n' roll to the world. "Rock Around the Clock" was even listed in the *Guinness Book of World Records* as the highest-selling rock 'n' roll single on vinyl of all time, with at least 25 million copies sold.

PART TWO:
THE BRITISH INVASION
(1960s)

Just as rock was gaining popularity among young Americans in the mid- to late-1950s, it had the same effect in the UK. Though some early British groups attempted to try to reproduce an American sound, others combined it with British style. This led to a surge of popularity among British rock musicians, pop music, and other cultural influences in the US in the mid-1960s—a phenomenon known as the British Invasion.

Most people consider the Beatles' February 1964 arrival in New York to be the beginning of the British Invasion. Their performance on *The Ed Sullivan Show* caused a cultural revolution, especially among young Americans, who welcomed—and even idolized—their innovative sound and look. This brought a wave of British musicians to the US, such as the Rolling Stones and the Who, gaining them notoriety and global acclaim.

The British Invasion of the 1960s expanded the definition and impact of rock music. Not only did it internationalize the genre and establish some of the most iconic rock legends in history, but it also shifted the focus of rock toward a group dynamic as opposed to a single performer.

[11]
THE BEATLES:
CHANGING THE WORLD

Just as Elvis Presley changed rock 'n' roll and the world as a solo performer, the Beatles did the same as a rock band. The "Fab Four" formed their group in Liverpool, England, in the late 1950s and early 1960s. Ultimately, the band consisted of John Lennon, Paul McCartney, George Harrison, and Ringo Starr.

Widely considered to be the most influential band of all time in terms of popular music and culture, the Beatles began their career with influences from 1950s rock 'n' roll and traditional pop, experimenting later with folk, psychedelia, and hard rock styles.

"Love Me Do" became the Beatles' first hit in 1962. By 1964, "Beatlemania" swept across the globe, making the band members international stars with both commercial and critical success. The group retreated from live performances in 1966 to focus on recording, resulting in iconic albums such as *Sgt. Pepper's Lonely Hearts Club Band* in 1967, *The White Album* in 1968, and *Abbey Road* in 1969. Though the group broke up in 1970, its members pursued solo careers with success. Unfortunately, John Lennon was assassinated in 1980, and George Harrison passed away from lung cancer in 2001.

The Beatles hold numerous records in terms of sales, singles, and album charts. They won seven Grammys, in addition to numerous other awards, and were inducted into the Rock & Roll Hall of Fame in 1988 — as soon as they were eligible. Each individual band member has been inducted, as well. The band's importance as far as music, performance, artistry, and culture is immeasurable, and their canon of songs will likely outlast the legacy of many other bands.

The Beatles undoubtedly changed the rock 'n' roll world and the music industry overall through their talented and pioneering songwriting, in addition to their groundbreaking experimentation in the studio. They also changed the world through their enduring impact on popular culture, particularly among young listeners in the 1960s.

The Beatles redefined the genre of rock, setting the foundation for the future of music groups, and the band will likely retain its reputation as the greatest in rock 'n' roll history.

[12]
THE ROLLING STONES:
THE BAD BOYS OF ROCK

The Rolling Stones were second only to the Beatles in terms of importance in the British Invasion, and many people consider the

Stones to be the greatest rock 'n' roll band of all time. Original members of the band include Mick Jagger, Keith Richards, Brian Jones, Ian Stewart, Bill Wyman, and Charlie Watts. However, it's the enduring creative partnership of Jagger as the band's frontman and Richards as guitarist that has produced some of the biggest rock 'n' roll classics of all time. Such songs include "Lady Jane," "Jumpin' Jack Flash," "Paint It, Black," and "(I Can't Get No) Satisfaction."

The Rolling Stones led a return to the rock 'n' roll' R&B roots with their initial covers of R&B music. The band formed in 1962 in London. At home in the UK and as part of the British Invasion of the 1960s, the Rolling Stones set the musical tone for what would later become known as hard rock. Their embrace of 1960s counterculture helped define generations of youth across the world. Mick Jagger, Keith Richards, and other bandmates also embodied and symbolized the life and image of rock stars, from celebrity treatment to certain excesses and absolute fan adoration. The Stones consistently pushed musical and social boundaries, including their refusal to perform in segregated venues in solidarity with the civil rights movement.

In many ways, the Rolling Stones were a foil for the Beatles, appealing to a more rebellious demographic with their rougher image and grittier sound, though their commercial and critical success rivaled the Fab Four during the British Invasion.

Throughout the decades, this "bad boy" group has consistently pioneered edgy performances with incredible rock songs. The Rolling Stones won three Grammy Awards and a Lifetime Achievement Award at the Grammys. In 1989, they were inducted into the Rock & Roll Hall of Fame.

Even as near octogenarians, the remaining members of the Stones are still selling out stadium tours, and their music will continue to be remembered by and impact generations in the future.

[13]
THE WHO:
ROCK OPERAS & DESTRUCTION

The Who formed in London in 1964. The British rock group consisted of Roger Daltrey on vocals, Pete Townshend on guitar, John Entwistle on bassist, and Keith Moon on drums from 1964–1978.

In addition to being part of the British Invasion of the 1960s, the Who made significant contributions to rock 'n' roll, influencing bands in the hard rock, punk, mod, and power pop genres. They implemented the Marshall stack amplifier system and use of synthesizers in their performances in addition to pioneering rock opera and instrument destruction in their act.

Hits such as "My Generation," "Substitute," and "I Can See for Miles" gained them popularity in both the US and UK, as did their performances at the Monterey Pop Festival in 1967, Woodstock, and Isle of Wight. The band was inducted into the Rock & Roll Hall of Fame in 1990.

In 1969, the Who famously put rock opera on the map with their groundbreaking fourth studio album, *Tommy*. Though technically not the first rock opera, the Who's double concept album paired rock music with lyrics to present a common story in a somewhat classical form. This pioneered the way for other legendary rock opera works such as *Bat Out of Hell* by Meat Loaf, *The Rise and Fall of Ziggy Stardust and the Spiders* by David Bowie, *The Wall* by Pink Floyd, and *American Idiot* by Green Day.

Tommy was a critical and commercial success upon release, launching the Who as international rock stars. It was later adapted as a Hollywood film in 1975 and a Broadway musical in 1992.

By most accounts, the Who was also the first well-known rock band to incorporate the "art" of instrument destruction—

something that characterized their live performances in the mid-1960s. In 1964, Pete Townshend started the trend at a tavern performance in London, during which he accidentally broke his guitar on the low ceiling of the venue. He then began smashing guitars on stage intentionally.

Keith Moon added to the band's destructive performance art by destroying drum kits at the end of some shows, memorably detonating explosives in his drums at the end of performing "My Generation" on the US television show *The Smothers Brothers Comedy Hour*.

Though instrument destruction can be expensive and poses the risks of injury, it has become fairly common among rock 'n' roll bands as a means of displaying emotion and creating a moment of drama for fans.

From impactful performances to legendary music and rock opera, the Who is one of the most influential bands in the British Invasion and rock history.

[14]
THE KINKS:
PIONEERS OF POWER CHORDS

The Kinks are considered an important and lasting influence as part of the British Invasion of the 1960s. Their 1964 hit, "You Really Got Me," pioneered the use of power chords, perfect fifths, and octaves, with the opening guitar riff played by Dave Davies and written by Ray Davies. The Davies brothers, from north London, added Peter Quaife as their bassist and Mick Avory on drums to form the Kinks. "You Really Got Me" was the band's third single, becoming a top hit in the UK and charting in the US soon after.

The Kinks were a significant part of the British Invasion but became entangled in a union dispute with the American

Federation of Musicians during their 1965 US tour. As a result, they were banned from making American appearances until 1969. However, they regained their US following—and then some—by touring after the ban was lifted and with the popular yet controversial release of "Lola" in 1970.

In 1979, the Kinks sold out Madison Square Garden, and their 1983 hit, "Come Dancing," has remained the band's highest-charting single in the US.

The Kinks' four original members were inducted into the Rock & Roll Hall of Fame in 1990, and their music continues to inspire musicians today. Their legacy stems not just from the now-classic power chords of "You Really Got Me" but from songs and concept albums addressing politics, pop culture, and education. The Kinks influenced stadium rock, heavy metal, and punk rock, including bands like the Who and Van Halen.

[15]
THE YARDBIRDS:
BIRTHPLACE OF GUITAR GODS

Formed in 1963 in London, The Yardbirds are considered the first guitar gods. In fact, this English band launched the careers of three legendary rock guitarists: Eric Clapton, Jeff Beck, and Jimmy Page. Other band members from the group's inception to their breakup in 1968 included Keith Relf (vocals, harmonica), Chris Dreja (guitar, bass), Jim McCarty (drums), and Paul Samwell-Smith (bass). The Yardbirds' range of music featured blues and pop, along with hard and psychedelic rock, with hits like "For Your Love," "Shapes of Things," and "Heart Full of Soul."

Eric Clapton joined the Yardbirds in late 1963 as lead guitarist based on his reputation in the R&B pub scene. Clapton remained with the band for 18 months before leaving to join John Mayall's

Bluesbreakers as the Yardbirds gravitated more toward commercial pop music.

In March of 1965, Jeff Beck replaced Eric Clapton in the Yardbirds and remained a key member of the band for nearly two years. Jimmy Page had played with Eric Clapton and Jeff Beck and reportedly suggested Beck as a replacement for Clapton after declining the offer himself. However, Page eventually joined the Yardbirds when Paul Samwell-Smith left, overlapping Beck's time with the band for a while. Though Clapton, Beck, and Page were all part of the Yardbirds, they never played together as part of the original group.

The band split up in 1968, with Relf and McCarty forming a group called Renaissance while Page formed Led Zeppelin. In 1992, the Yardbirds were inducted into the Rock & Roll Hall of Fame, and their influence as part of the British Invasion and blues rock genre continues today. In addition to three rock-star guitarists as former band members, the Yardbirds developed a style that allowed for instrumental jams and improvisation rather than simple repetition. This fostered subgenres such as garage, hard, progressive, and acid rock and cemented the guitar's supremacy in rock 'n' roll.

[16]
THE ANIMALS:
"HOUSE OF THE RISING SUN"

The Animals, formed in 1962 in Newcastle, England, were a big part of the British Invasion in the mid-1960s. The group brought a distinctive blues sound to their music, reinventing songs such as "House of the Rising Sun." Original band members included Eric Burdon (vocals), Chas Chandler (bass), John Steel (drums), Alan Price (keyboard), and Hilton Valentine (guitar). Hit songs like "We Gotta Get Out of This Place" and "Don't Let Me Be Misunderstood" and intense live performances reflected the counterculture of the decade and the changes facing young people in Britain and across the world.

In 1964, The Animals' "House of the Rising Sun" became an international hit. The Animals used the song while touring with Chuck Berry to close out their performance and distinguish themselves with audiences. The Animals recorded the song in London between tour dates — in one take.

The Animals' contemporary rock arrangement transformed the traditional American folk song into a haunting ballad that's still listed as one of the greatest songs of all time. It's also the song's most commercially-successful version, though it wasn't included on an album but issued as a single.

Many consider the Animals' recording of "House of the Rising Sun" to be the first folk rock hit or classic rock song. Ultimately, "House of the Rising Sun" was a breakout hit for the Animals and the first number-one song of the British Invasion that had nothing to do with the Beatles.

Unfortunately, the Animals split up in 1966 due to management issues and internal conflict. Burdon formed a new band called Eric Burdon and the Animals, finding some success in the genres of psychedelic and progressive rock; however, that group dissolved at the end of the 1960s.

The Animals' original members were inducted into the Rock & Roll Hall of Fame in 1994, though they did not perform, and Burdon was not in attendance. Their music is still well-known today, impacting various rock genres, and the Animals are credited with influencing artists, from the band Genesis to Bruce Springsteen and Bob Dylan — who recorded his own version of "House of the Rising Sun" in 1961.

[17]
ICONIC PERFORMANCE: THE BEATLES AT SHEA STADIUM

The Beatles performed at Shea Stadium in New York City on August 15, 1964. A documentary film shows 50 minutes of the band's concert and other footage from the height of "Beatlemania" in the United States. Bob Precht directed and produced the documentary, along with NEMS Enterprises and Subafilms. Though the Beatles made other stops on their American tour that year, their Shea Stadium performance is considered the first major stadium concert in rock 'n' roll history.

More than 55,000 people attended the concert, and screams from the audience drowned out the music. Heightened security had to attend to fainting fans and people trying to rush the stage.

The Shea Stadium concert broke records for concert attendance, launching the concept of a stadium show for future artists and audiences. The Beatles made $300,000—equal to more than $3 million today—for their Shea Stadium performance, reflecting the band's musical and cultural importance in America and across the world.

Though the Beatles retired from commercial concerts and touring in 1966 to focus on studio-produced records, their memorable performance at Shea Stadium paved the way for many developments in the music industry—from concert venues in sports arenas to improved sound equipment. Like many precedents set by the "Fab Four," the Shea Stadium concert remains an iconic moment for fans and rock historians alike.

[18]
LANDMARK ALBUM:
THE BEATLES' *SGT. PEPPER'S LONELY HEARTS CLUB BAND*

When the Beatles released the album *Sgt. Pepper's Lonely Hearts Club Band* in May 1967, rock 'n' roll would never be the same. This album served as a landmark in everything from unique sound and technology to iconic cover art. The album launched hits such as "Lovely Rita," "Getting Better," "Lucy in the Sky with Diamonds," "A Day in the Life," and "With a Little Help from My Friends." *Sgt. Pepper* also marked the Beatles' transition from the "Fab Four" pop group to mature, innovative artists who reflected the counterculture of the time and were willing to push beyond the traditions of rock albums.

Sgt. Pepper was recorded at Abbey Road Studios and took about six months. In addition to unprecedented studio time, the Beatles took risks, multitracking and blending styles like pop, jazz, and psychedelic rock. Many consider *Sgt. Pepper* to be the first concept album, though the group didn't necessarily intend an overall theme. Consequently, the record inspired future concept albums, including Pink Floyd's *The Dark Side of the Moon*.

The first of the Beatles' albums to be released globally at the same time, this landmark album went on to become the bestselling UK record of all time. *Sgt. Pepper's Lonely Hearts Club Band* directly established an artistic foundation for future rock musicians and movements in the genre, including stage alter egos embraced by artists such as David Bowie, concept and other album formats, an occult presence embraced by groups such as the Rolling Stones, and even the beginnings of glam rock. As the Beatles' eighth studio album, *Sgt. Pepper's Lonely Hearts Club Band* only further cemented the group's legendary status among the greatest rock bands in history.

[19]
THE IMPACT OF BRITISH BLUES: JOHN MAYALL & THE BLUESBREAKERS

John Mayall—often referred to as the father of British blues—and his band, the Bluesbreakers, helped develop an English urban sound and revive R&B in rock 'n' roll in the late 1960s. Led by Mayall, the Bluesbreakers is often referred to as an "incubator" for British talent, including musicians who would go on to become some of the most famous in rock history, such as Eric Clapton, Mick Fleetwood, Mick Taylor, Jon Mark, and John Almond.

Born in 1933 in central England, John Mayall played piano, blues harmonica, guitar, and keyboard, in addition to performing vocals with his distinct voice. His father played guitar and banjo and influenced Mayall with his collection of boogie piano records.

Mayall moved to London in 1962, forming the group that would become the Bluesbreakers in 1963. The band featured a number of members who would come and go due in part to the freedom Mayall allowed his bandmates. He moved to the US in 1968, disbanding the Bluesbreakers, though he continued to perform and release music with albums like *The Turning Point*.

In 1982, Mayall re-formed the Bluesbreakers, though membership remained fluid. The Bluesbreakers name was retired by Mayall in 2008, and in 2013, he formed the John Mayall Band.

Mayall earned two Grammy nominations and was selected for the Rock & Roll Hall of Fame in 2024. His 1966 album *Blues Breakers with Eric Clapton* is considered one of the greatest in the British blues genre to this day.

[20]
THE RISE OF PSYCHEDELIA: PINK FLOYD'S EARLY DAYS

The quick popularity of psychedelic rock that began on the US West Coast in the late 1960s made its way to Britain just as rapidly. British bands, from the Beatles to the Who and the Rolling Stones, joined the movement, incorporating experimental elements in their music. British psychedelia was, to some degree, less edgy than American "acid rock," focusing more on the surreal, and tended to stick within traditional pop song structures.

Pink Floyd was at the top of the emerging psychedelic scene in the mid-1960s UK. In 1967, the band released its first album, *The Piper at the Gates of Dawn*, featuring groundbreaking, experimental songs, and many consider the album to be Pink Floyd's quintessential psychedelic work. This was primarily because of Syd Barrett's songwriting, which included surreal lyrics and distinct instrumental effects.

Before the album's release, Pink Floyd headlined the counterculture fundraiser 14-Hour Technicolor Dream. Such icons as John Lennon and Andy Warhol attended this London concert, which featured artistic legends along with many underground British psychedelic bands.

Unfortunately, Barrett's drug use and alleged mental illness caused the members of Pink Floyd to replace him with David Gilmour in 1968. Pink Floyd moved away from psychedelia somewhat soon after, but their psychedelic roots and imprint on the genre and the counterculture it represented still remain.

PART THREE: THE AMERICAN COUNTERPART (1960S)

The 1960s was as important a decade for American rock 'n' roll as it was for British rock bands making their way overseas. The American counterpart to the British Invasion demonstrated a diversity of sound and style that reflected the social consciousness of the decade and a rapid evolution of rock music across the country. In fact, rock 'n' roll became a symbol of the counterculture, serving as a vehicle for significant political and social change in the US.

In the 1960s, the youth of America brought about a cultural revolution based on challenging tradition and advocacy for equality, peace, and freedom. Events such as Woodstock and the Summer of Love, as well as legendary artists from Bob Dylan and Jimi Hendrix to the Grateful Dead, brought counterculture movements to the forefront of American consciousness while redefining rock music and its impact on the transformation of global culture.

Between the British Invasion and America's contribution to rock music, the 1960s will likely remain the most influential decade in rock 'n' roll history, as well as art and pop culture overall.

[21]
BOB DYLAN:
ROCK'S POET LAUREATE

Bob Dylan's music and poetic lyrics helped define America's youth culture in the 1960s, and his work continues to impact musicians, writers, artists, and audiences across the globe. Dylan fused rock instrumentation with folk music, pushing creative boundaries by incorporating political counterculture and social consciousness—as well as poetry and literature—into popular music.

Dylan was born Robert Zimmerman in May of 1941 in Duluth, Minnesota. He was heavily influenced by the folk songs of Woody Guthrie, in addition to blues and country music. In 1963, he released his second studio album, *The Freewheelin' Bob Dylan*, which featured "Blowin' in the Wind" — a song that became a protest anthem and symbol of cultural revolution. Dylan's 1964 release of "The Times They Are A-Changin'" solidified his cultural and political importance as part of the anti-war and civil rights movements.

In addition to popularizing folk rock, Dylan produced albums in the country and contemporary gospel genres. Even as an octogenarian, he continues to create and perform.

Bob Dylan has achieved an unprecedented number of accolades and awards throughout the 20th and 21st centuries, including several Grammys, an Academy Award, and the Presidential Medal of Freedom. He won a Pulitzer Prize special citation in 2008 and is an inductee of the Rock & Roll Hall of Fame, as well as the Songwriters Hall of Fame. Dylan received the Nobel Prize in Literature in 2016 for his lyricism and poetic expression.

An iconic voice of his generation, Bob Dylan will be remembered as the poet laureate of rock 'n' roll, as well as one of the most influential singer-songwriters in history.

[22]
THE BEACH BOYS: CALIFORNIA SOUND

The Beach Boys were founded in 1961 by three brothers — Brian, Dennis, and Carl Wilson — along with their cousin, Mike Love, and friend Al Jardine in Hawthorne, California. Their unique vocal harmonies soon came to represent the sun, surfing, and youth culture of Southern California, though the band's success extended much farther than the West Coast across the decades.

The Beach Boys started as a garage band managed by the Wilson brother's father, Murry Wilson. They signed with Capitol Records and released their debut album, *Surfin' Safari*, in 1962.

Early hits such as "California Girls," "Surfin' U.S.A.," "I Get Around," and "Fun, Fun, Fun" solidified the group's place as one of the most popular rock bands in America — even up against the decade's British Invasion.

The 1966 album *Pet Sounds* departed from the Beach Boys' usual lyrical themes and musical orchestration, but it remains one of the most important and innovative records in rock history.

With their quintessential sound, catalog of hit songs, and influential composition and recording techniques, the Beach Boys remain a quintessential American rock band and are known around the globe. They're consistently featured among the greatest artists of all time and were inducted into the Rock & Roll Hall of Fame in 1988.

Though their songs may sound simple and nostalgic, the Beach Boys are critically acclaimed for their music, which captured an entire region and inspired generations of listeners and artists within many genres of rock.

[23]
JIMI HENDRIX: GUITAR LEGEND

Jimi Hendrix is not only considered a guitar legend — he's also among the most creative and impactful musicians in rock history. He was born Johnny Allen Hendrix in November 1942 in Seattle, Washington. His father, James "Al" Hendrix, recognized his son's deep interest in music and the guitar. Al bought a secondhand guitar in 1958, though his son couldn't read or write music, and Jimi taught himself to play.

Hendrix enlisted in the US Army in 1961, earning the "Screaming Eagles" patch as a paratrooper. After he was discharged, he played with several artists, including Sam Cooke, Ike and Tina Turner, and Little Richard.

In 1966, Chas Chandler, former bassist of the Animals, signed Hendrix and helped him form the Jimi Hendrix Experience in London. The band's first album, *Are You Experienced*, is one of the most popular psychedelic rock albums in history. Songs such as "Purple Haze," "Foxy Lady," and "Fire," along with Hendrix's festival performances, launched him as a global guitarist and rock star.

By 1968, Hendrix had built his own New York City recording studio and faced short but demanding years of creating and performing his music while expanding his vision and influence.

Jimi Hendrix created new, innovative methods of playing the electric guitar, and though his music career was cut short by his death in September of 1970 at the age of 27, his solo contributions to rock music are nearly unparalleled. His performance at Woodstock in August of 1969 remains iconic — particularly his rendition of "The Star-Spangled Banner."

Just over a year later, musicians and the public were shocked and saddened to learn of Hendrix's passing, reportedly due to a drug overdose. However, his guitar-playing prowess, innovative style, and cultural significance continue to influence musicians and fans alike. Hendrix was inducted into the Rock & Roll Hall of Fame in 1992.

[24]
JANIS JOPLIN:
THE QUEEN OF PSYCHEDELIC SOUL

Janis Joplin was an important figure and contributor to the blues revival and psychedelic sound of San Francisco rock in the 1960s. Joplin was born in 1943 and grew up in Texas; she then made her way to the Haight-Ashbury area of San Francisco as a young singer-songwriter in the mid-1960s. Her music was influenced by blues, soul, and gospel.

Joplin's distinctive voice and soulful style conveyed both strength and vulnerability. Janis Joplin was the first queen of rock 'n' roll, and though her career was tragically short, she has inspired generations of female singers and artists.

In 1966, Joplin joined Big Brother and the Holding Company, a psychedelic rock band that rose out of the San Francisco music scene of 1965. In 1967, with Janis Joplin as the lead singer, Big Brother and the Holding Company distinguished themselves at the Monterey Pop Festival, leading to a contract with Columbia Records.

In 1968, the band released *Cheap Thrills*, with the iconic track "Piece of My Heart" — Joplin's most popular recording. *Cheap Thrills* hit number one on the Billboard charts and is considered quintessential among the psychedelic albums to come out of San Francisco at the time.

In 1968, Janis Joplin left Big Brother and the Holding Company to pursue a solo career. She formed a back-up group called the Kozmic Blues Band, which showcased her roots in soul and blues.

Though Joplin's music career was cut short due to a heroin overdose in 1970, her voice remains iconic as the queen of psychedelic soul. Janis Joplin was not only a musical pioneer and symbol of 1960s rock, but she also paved the way for women in rock 'n' roll and their contributions to song, sound, and style. In 1995, she was inducted posthumously into the Rock & Roll Hall of Fame.

[25]
THE DOORS:
DARK AND BROODING

The Doors emerged as one of the most important Los Angeles bands of the late 1960s and one of the most influential rock groups of all time. Iconic songs such as "Light My Fire," "Break on Through (to the Other Side)," "People Are Strange," "Hello, I Love You," and "Riders on the Storm" are as inspirational today as they were over five decades ago.

The Doors were influenced by jazz, blues, psychedelia, and poetry, which contributed to the brooding mystique and appeal of frontman Jim Morrison. At a time when rock music often advocated for peace and love, the Doors produced a catalog of hits that confronted the status quo and challenged their audience.

The Doors' history began when Jim Morrison and keyboardist Ray Manzarek met at UCLA's film school, then again at Venice Beach in the summer of 1965. Manzarek asked Morrison to join his current band, though Morrison considered himself more of a poet than a singer. Guitarist Robby Krieger and drummer John Densmore joined Manzarek and Morrison soon after, and the Doors released their first self-titled album in January of 1967 with Elektra Records. The band's name is derived from Aldous Huxley's 1954 autobiographical book, *The Doors of Perception*, based on his psychedelic experiences. The Doors released six successful studio albums that led to classic hit singles and a large fanbase.

Unfortunately, the band's live performances became controversial due to Jim Morrison's erratic and "scandalous" behavior, as well as drug and alcohol use. In 1967, Morrison was arrested on stage for obscene and indecent behavior and again in 1969 for "lewd" behavior at a concert in Florida.

After the release of the band's last album, *LA Woman*, Morrison moved to Paris in 1971, where he died. His death, attributed to cardiac arrest, marked the end of the Doors, though the group's remaining members continued their musical and artistic careers.

The Doors were inducted into the Rock & Roll Hall of Fame in 1993, and their contributions to rock 'n' roll are considered legendary in their musical creativity, brooding poetic lyrics, and rebellious artistry.

[26]
THE GRATEFUL DEAD: PSYCHEDELIC PIONEERS

The Grateful Dead formed in 1965 in San Francisco. Members originally included Jerry Garcia on lead guitar, Phil Lesh on bass, Bob Weir on rhythm guitar, and Bill Kreutzmann on drums. Though the band first had more of an acoustic folk style, they transitioned to electric instruments and became pioneers of psychedelic rock. This was aided in part by the Dead's participation in the Acid Tests of the mid-1960s—parties and free-form performances organized by Ken Kesey, author of *One Flew Over the Cuckoo's Nest*, in San Francisco. The Acid Tests centered on the use of and advocacy for LSD, the psychedelic drug commonly known as "acid," which was legal in California until late 1966. The drug was offered to performers and audience members to "enhance" the experience.

The Grateful Dead popularized exploratory music, improvisation, and unique live performances in addition to blending multiple genres, including folk, jazz, country, and classical. Their free, spontaneous performances and concerts that popped up around San Francisco helped spread word-of-mouth praise for the Dead, heightening the band's popularity.

Warner Brothers signed the Grateful Dead, and their first self-titled album was released in 1967, though their studio recordings often went beyond radio-play length and didn't quite measure up to their live performances.

The Grateful Dead's psychedelic and experimental music led to a cult following that came to be known as "Deadheads," dedicated to following the band's touring schedule in the early 1970s and beyond.

In keeping with their emphasis on artistic expression through live performance, the Dead allowed audience members to record bootleg copies of their concerts as a way to share their music. The Grateful Dead's successful tours, albums, and memorable live performances continued until Jerry Garcia's death in 1995.

The Dead's psychedelic roots influenced many of their contemporaries in the 1960s, but their legacy also encompasses a variety of musical styles and beloved improvisational performances.

[27]
ICONIC PERFORMANCE: JIMI HENDRIX AT WOODSTOCK

Woodstock featured several legendary rock artists, yet Jimi Hendrix's performance is widely considered the 1969 festival's most iconic. He took the stage on Monday, August 18, after much of the crowd had left. Hendrix began his set by flashing the peace sign and playing "The Star-Spangled Banner" on his guitar. His unconventional rendition of the national anthem featured crackles of feedback and distortion meant to evoke a sense of warfare, likely as a protest of America's involvement in Vietnam and other societal ills, such as racism.

Jimi Hendrix was famously critical of US politics, both at home and abroad. Having served with the 101st Airborne Division and honorably discharged about a year later, Hendrix understood what military commitment meant in the 1960s and that the complex political system was often indifferent to youth and people of color despite their sacrifices.

His instrumentation of the national anthem is iconic, not only for its display of his legendary talent but also for his ability to convey social commentary and support for American counterculture as the future.

Hendrix was not the first musician to play "The Star-Spangled Banner" in a nontraditional manner. Additionally, since he was the final act and the festival was not televised, comparatively few people saw his performance. It was only the release of the documentary film about Woodstock in March 1970 that would give people the opportunity to see Hendrix's version.

Of course, many Americans consider his iconic performance to be unpatriotic or irreverent, even today. However, considering the context of Woodstock, the role of rock music as a vehicle for activism at the time, and Jimi Hendrix's personal experiences and viewpoints—not to mention his visible emotion while playing—certainly make any "unpatriotic" label reductive and unjustified.

[28]
LANDMARK ALBUM:
THE BEACH BOYS' *PET SOUNDS*

Released in May of 1966, *Pet Sounds* was the Beach Boys' eleventh studio record. This landmark album, pioneered by Brian Wilson, not only redefined the Beach Boys as more than a "California" band but also revolutionized what pop-rock musicians could achieve in terms of sound, lyrics, production, and artistry.

Brian Wilson was the visionary behind *Pet Sounds* in terms of its ambitious, experimental, and progressive musical concept. Wilson worked with Tony Asher as a lyricist, and their collaboration led to complex arrangements of instruments, percussion, and vocal harmony.

Wilson was inspired by Phil Spector and his "Wall of Sound" technique, as well as the Beatles' 1965 release of *Rubber Soul*. With the use of "doubling" for traditional and unconventional instruments, as well as harmonic vocals, *Pet Sounds* is credited with the launch of progressive pop and the development of art rock.

Though *Pet Sounds* was not hugely successful in the US at the time of release—likely due to its departure from the Beach Boys' previous ten albums—it was soon recognized both commercially and critically as an achievement in musical innovation.

The Beatles acknowledged *Pet Sounds* as an inspiration for their album *Sgt. Pepper* and its legacy and impact in progressive pop music endures. Songs like "Wouldn't It Be Nice," "God Only Knows," and "Sloop John B" resonate with meaningful themes, cultural relevance, and emotional connection to listeners nearly six decades later.

In many ways, *Pet Sounds*, Brian Wilson, and the Beach Boys changed how rock musicians and audiences perceived the very concept of an album—making it much more than just a grouping of individual songs.

[29]
THE SUMMER OF LOVE: SAN FRANCISCO'S MUSIC SCENE

The Summer of Love in 1967 made San Francisco an essential part of the music scene of the 1960s and the primary location for advocates of social change. The movement was inspired by Jack Kerouac and other "Beat" authors and poets, as young people from across the country gathered in the Haight-Ashbury district and Golden Gate Park to form a counterculture community based on a rejection of materialism and conformity.

The phrase "Summer of Love" came from the Council for the Summer of Love, which was formed in the spring of 1967 by members who'd anticipated the crowds of people and potential problems facing San Francisco that summer. They supported a free clinic and coordinated housing, sanitation, and food with churches and other groups—though this didn't prevent the poor conditions, homelessness, and crime caused by factors like overcrowding and drug use. They also organized counterculture music and art performances.

Though local politicians and others attempted to stall the influx of "hippies," their efforts instead brought national media attention to the movement and activities in San Francisco.

In addition to the diverse music groups popping up and playing in San Francisco, the Summer of Love also saw two significant events that attracted large crowds and further enhanced the experience of those who traveled to that area.

The Fantasy Fair, Magic Mountain Music Festival, and the Monterey Pop Festival took place in June of 1967. These festivals introduced bands such as the Who, Jimi Hendrix Experience, Grateful Dead, and Janis Joplin with Big Brother and the Holding Company to a wide audience of young listeners.

[30]
WOODSTOCK 1969: THE FESTIVAL THAT DEFINED AN ERA

The 1960s revealed deep divisions and unrest across America. The Vietnam War was controversial on many levels, as were the civil rights movement and other issues that led to public conflict and violence, from riots to assassinations. Counterculture and anti-establishment sentiment grew among young Americans, who recognized the failures within the traditional political system and the detrimental effects of capitalism and social conformity. This social awareness and cultural growth converged at Woodstock in 1969 with some of the most impactful musicians and important rock music in history.

The Woodstock Music and Art Fair, commonly referred to as "Woodstock," took place in August 1969 at a farm in Bethel, New York. Though many logistical problems and unanticipated complications arose due to the size of the crowd, inclement weather, and limited resources, the festival ultimately proved a

42

peaceful and joyful experience for attendees and performers alike.

No one could have predicted the legendary music, interest in radical change, and commitment to humanity reflected in this event. Though many view Woodstock through a nostalgic lens, it set an important precedent for the relationship between rock music and reform.

Woodstock 1969 may have appeared to outsiders as a hedonistic, rebellious gathering of hippies and irreverent musicians; however, the festival epitomized the turmoil of the 1960s while defining an era of social, political, and cultural awakening. The entire event was far more than the sum of what has become its cliché parts: sex, drugs, and rock 'n' roll.

Artists used their performances as a form of social commentary and a call to political action. Festival attendees found opportunities for solidarity, expression, and community among fellow counterculture individuals from diverse areas and marginalized backgrounds. In the end, Woodstock's message of spiritual freedom, peace, and love, combined with music and art, marked a generation.

PART FOUR:
ROCK 'N' ROLL
EXPANSION (1970s)

The 1970s saw expansion and transformation in the rock 'n' roll genre, from legendary artists to music that remains influential today. Rock music further diversified into unique subgenres with experimental sounds and unique blends of styles. Progressive rock and glam rock not only pushed musical boundaries but societal norms as well, paving a path for punk and new wave to follow. Hard rock and heavy metal became popular, along with funk and art rock, incorporating elements of electronic, jazz, and classical music.

Legendary bands such as Led Zeppelin, Queen, and Pink Floyd emerged in the 1970s, and established groups like the Rolling Stones evolved in their music and performances. This decade of experimentation redefined the genre and subgenres of rock 'n' roll, producing some of the most iconic and deeply influential music of all time.

[31]
LED ZEPPELIN:
THE HEAVYWEIGHTS

When the Yardbirds broke up in 1968, guitarist Jimmy Page formed what was initially called the New Yardbirds with John Bonham (drums), Robert Plant (vocals), and John Paul Jones (bass, keyboards) in London. Reportedly, Keith Moon mentioned that it would fall like a "lead zeppelin," which resulted in Led Zeppelin being the group's name. Led Zeppelin became one of the most important bands in rock 'n' roll history, paving a path for hard rock, heavy metal, and stadium rock.

Their 1969 albums *Led Zeppelin* and *Led Zeppelin II* were popular, with hits such as "Dazed and Confused" and "Whole Lotta Love." In 1971, Led Zeppelin released their fourth, untitled album, featuring legendary songs such as "Black Dog," "Rock and Roll," and the iconic "Stairway to Heaven." The commercial success of Led Zeppelin's music resulted in tours that broke records but also left the band with a reputation for partying and wild behavior. The group disbanded in 1980 after Bonham's death, though their rock image and music continue to impact pop culture.

Led Zeppelin is considered one of the greatest bands of all time in terms of sales, innovation, and influence. In 1995, they were inducted into the Rock & Roll Hall of Fame, and bands from the genres of hard rock, heavy metal, punk, and alternative rock have credited Led Zeppelin with inspiration for their music. Some of these groups include Rush, Queen, Aerosmith, Megadeth, the Ramones, Nirvana, and Pearl Jam.

Music historians note Led Zeppelin's influence on album-oriented rock and for pioneering arena/stadium concerts as well. In 2005, they received a Grammy Lifetime Achievement Award, and in 2012, they received Kennedy Center Honors.

Led Zeppelin will continue to be known as rock 'n' roll heavyweights as their music continues to be appreciated by generations to come.

[32]
BLACK SABBATH:
FOUNDERS OF HEAVY METAL

Black Sabbath was formed in 1968 in Birmingham, England. Led by vocalist Ozzy Osbourne, other band members include Tony Iommi (guitar), Geezer Butler (bass), and Bill Ward (drums). The band is credited with creating and defining the heavy metal genre with their 1970 albums *Black Sabbath* and *Paranoid* and 1971's *Master of Reality*. Black Sabbath's music features horror and occult themes, and though the band was commercially successful, it took some time for critics to give them positive reviews.

In 1979, Osbourne was fired from Black Sabbath due to substance abuse. The band went through high turnover among members, though guitarist Iommi remained a consistent presence.

In 1997, Black Sabbath's original members reunited for a live album and occasional tours until 2005. After another reunion in 2011, they played their final concert together in 2017. In addition to being founders of heavy metal, the band set roots for many metal subgenres, such as sludge, black, doom, and thrash.

Black Sabbath is considered one of the most commercially-successful heavy metal bands and among the greatest artists of all time. They were inducted into the Rock & Roll Hall of Fame in 2006 and have won two Grammys, along with a Grammy Lifetime Achievement Award in 2019.

Their impact on heavy metal music and hard rock is legendary, with the hit "Iron Man" ranked among the greatest metal songs of all time. Bands such as Metallica, Nirvana, Van Halen, Foo Fighters, Judas Priest, and Guns N' Roses have credited Black Sabbath with influencing their music, and Ozzy Osbourne, in particular, remains an icon of pop culture.

[33]
QUEEN: THEATRICAL AND POWERFUL

Queen was formed in London by frontman Freddie Mercury (vocals, piano), Brian May (guitar, vocals), and Roger Taylor (drums, vocals) in 1970. Bassist John Deacon joined the following year. Queen is a legendary rock band with roots in progressive and hard rock, along with heavy metal. Eventually, they became known for arena and pop rock, with lasting anthems such as 1977's "We Are the Champions" and "We Will Rock You" still mainstays at sporting events around the world.

The band released their first albums in 1973 and 1974, *Queen* and *Queen II*. By 1975, the band was an international success, particularly with their unique single "Bohemian Rhapsody" and its accompanying music video.

In the 1980s, Queen was one of the most popular stadium rock bands, and their performance at Live Aid in 1985 is considered one of the greatest in rock 'n' roll history. Freddie Mercury was diagnosed with AIDS in 1987, though he didn't reveal his condition publicly until the day before he died in November 1991. In 2004, May and Taylor joined with vocalists Adam Lambert and Paul Rodgers, touring as Queen+.

Queen has been an integral part of music and pop culture for decades, including the iconic sing-along car scene with "Bohemian Rhapsody" in the movie *Wayne's World*. They're among the bestselling music artists of all time and were inducted into the Rock & Roll Hall of Fame in 2001. In 2018, they received the Grammy Lifetime Achievement Award. Freddie Mercury's powerful voice and the band's vast catalog of memorable songs will continue to inspire and influence future rock musicians and bands.

[34]
DAVID BOWIE:
THE CHAMELEON OF ROCK

David Bowie was born David Robert Jones in January 1947. His music career is one of the most acclaimed and influential in both rock 'n' roll history and pop culture.

David Bowie became a professional musician in 1963 but didn't achieve popular success until releasing "Space Oddity" in 1969. By the 1970s, Bowie had become an integral part of the glam rock scene with his alter ego, Ziggy Stardust, developed from his popular 1972 single "Starman" and album *The Rise and Fall of Ziggy Stardust and the Spiders from Mars*.

In 1975, Bowie found success in the US with the album *Young Americans* and the hit single "Fame." Just two years later, he collaborated with Brian Eno in what became known as the Berlin Trilogy, followed by the commercially and critically successful albums *Heroes* in 1977 and *Lodger* in 1979.

David Bowie's popularity peaked in the 1980s with hits such as the 1981 collaboration with Queen "Under Pressure" and 1983's "Let's Dance." Besides taking on acting roles in movies and television, Bowie also recorded a Christmas duet with Bing Crosby in 1977, "Peace on Earth/Little Drummer Boy," which has become a holiday classic. David Bowie died from liver cancer in 2016.

Bowie will be long remembered for his innovation, experimentation, and reinvention—earning him the nickname "chameleon of rock." He's one of the bestselling musicians of all time, earning six Grammys, among other awards. In 1996, David Bowie was inducted into the Rock & Roll Hall of Fame.

His musical talent and ambition have influenced numerous artists as well as music genres, and he's considered a leader in bringing intellectual concepts and avant-garde performances into the world of rock music. David Bowie will remain a legendary rock star and pop culture icon.

[35]
PINK FLOYD:
MASTERS OF PSYCHEDELIA
& MORE

Pink Floyd was founded in 1965 in London by Syd Barrett (vocals, guitar), Roger Waters (vocals, bass guitar), Richard Wright (vocals, keyboards), and Nick Mason (drums). David Gilmour joined in 1967, and Barrett left the next year due to mental health issues.

Pink Floyd is known as one of the first psychedelic rock groups in the UK because of their experimental recordings and live shows. They're also considered one of the greatest progressive rock bands in history.

From 1973 to 1980, Pink Floyd enjoyed enormous success with legendary albums such as *The Dark Side of the Moon*, *Wish You Were Here*, *Animals*, and *The Wall*. Due to tensions and difficulties, Wright left the band in 1981, and Waters exited in 1985. Wright later returned to the band but passed away in 2008. Barrett passed away in 2006.

Pink Floyd has sold over 250 million records, and their works consistently appear on greatest-of-all-time lists. In 1996, Pink Floyd was inducted into the Rock & Roll Hall of Fame. Their artistic influence continues to affect rock music across many subgenres. Musicians and bands such as David Bowie, U2, Queen, Nine Inch Nails, and Radiohead have all credited Pink Floyd as inspiration for their own music.

The themes of alienation, isolation, conflict, and institutional oppression characterizing Pink Floyd's music and their mastery of creation remain an important part of rock music's canon.

[36]
AEROSMITH:
BAD BOYS FROM BOSTON

Aerosmith formed in Boston, Massachusetts, in 1970. Band members include Steven Tyler (vocals), Joe Perry (guitar), Joey Kramer (drums), Brad Whitford (guitar), and Tom Hamilton (bass.) Aerosmith enjoyed huge success in the 1970s with their hit songs "Sweet Emotion," "Dream On," and "Walk This Way," in addition to their six multiplatinum albums released that decade. With their unique blend of blues, hard rock, heavy metal, glam metal, and pop, Aerosmith became globally popular and was often referred to as "America's Greatest Rock and Roll Band."

The band also earned the nickname "The Bad Boys of Boston," in part due to their notoriously excessive lifestyle, substance abuse, and internal conflicts.

Between 1979 and 1981, Perry and Whitford left the group, and Aerosmith faced setbacks in terms of popularity and success. Perry and Whitford reunited with Aerosmith in 1984, yet it was the group's collaboration with Run-D.M.C. on the remake of "Walk This Way" in 1986 that set off their unprecedented comeback.

Aerosmith's 1987 album *Permanent Vacation* set them on a renewed path of musical awards and commercial success that continues today.

In addition to being one of the bestselling rock bands of all time, Aerosmith has pioneered groundbreaking projects, from iconic concept music videos to movie and television appearances and video games such as "Guitar Hero: Aerosmith."

In 1999, Walt Disney World opened an Aerosmith-themed roller coaster. Aerosmith has collaborated with a variety of rock and non-rock artists besides Run-D.M.C., including Eminem, Carrie Underwood, Alice Cooper, and Nelly, for a Super Bowl halftime show.

Though the band has retired from touring, they remain one of the most influential bands in rock history. Aerosmith has won numerous awards, including four Grammys, and the band was inducted into the Rock & Roll Hall of Fame in 2001. Their music consistently appears on greatest-of-all-time lists. Groups such as Guns N' Roses, Skid Row, Warrant, the Black Crowes, Metallica, Nirvana, and Pearl Jam have all acknowledged the impact of Aerosmith on their music.

Aerosmith represents what many people consider the epitome of rock 'n' roll, from their rebellious image to legendary performances and classic songs.

[37]
ICONIC PERFORMANCE: LED ZEPPELIN AT MADISON SQUARE GARDEN

In the summer of 1973, Led Zeppelin performed for three nights at New York City's Madison Square Garden (MSG.) This led to a concert film and the soundtrack album *The Song Remains the Same*, released in 1976. Joe Massot directed the film, which was funded by the band, and within a week, Massot was able to assemble everything to record Led Zeppelin's MSG performances on July 27, 28, and 29, 1973.

Though problematic in many ways, the film captured iconic moments of the band's stage presence and talent in addition to the infamous theft of Led Zeppelin's money — which was never recovered — from a safe deposit box at New York's Drake Hotel.

The recording of these concerts had some continuity problems, including confusing shifts in John Paul Jones's and Jimmy Page's wardrobe — which turned out to be footage from an earlier performance at a different venue. Despite this, the band recreated the Madison Square Garden concert in 1974 with a mock-up set in Shepperton Studios.

By the time *The Song Remains the Same* was released, the film was nearly two years behind schedule and had far exceeded its original budget. Though it was successful at the box office, the film was criticized by many, who cited its amateur technical production and self-indulgent style and content.

Ultimately, the recording of Led Zeppelin's concerts at Madison Square Garden — in addition to other material — made these live performances accessible to fans. Not only did it capture the band's talents at the pinnacle of their popularity, but it also showcased the excess and "show business" of the rock-star lifestyle.

53

[38]
LANDMARK ALBUM: PINK FLOYD'S
THE DARK SIDE OF THE MOON

Pink Floyd's eighth album, *The Dark Side of the Moon,* was released in March 1973. The introspective concept album was intended to reflect the pressures of the members' rock-star lifestyle and address former band member Syd Barrett's mental health issues.

The Dark Side of the Moon encompasses not only themes of mental illness but also greed, death, time, and conflict. The singles "Money" and "Us and Them" promoted the album, and the record cover, a prismatic spectrum designed by Storm Thorgerson, remains an iconic image of rock 'n' roll.

The Dark Side of the Moon was not only Pink Floyd's bestselling release but also the bestselling record of the 1970s and among the top bestsellers in history. In 1999, the record was inducted into the Grammy Hall of Fame, and in 2012, its significance led the Library of Congress to select the album for preservation in the US National Recording Registry. It brought critical acclaim and global fame to Pink Floyd and is considered a landmark in the history of rock music and a touchstone of what many call the album era.

The legacy of *The Dark Side of the Moon* is still felt today, from cover versions of the album's songs to its influence on artists like David Bowie and Radiohead.

[39]
THE BIRTH OF ARENA ROCK: KISS AND ALICE COOPER

Arena rock took root in the mid-1970s with groups such as Queen, Aerosmith, Led Zeppelin, KISS, and Alice Cooper. These bands and others developed large-scale production concerts performed for thousands of fans in huge venues like stadiums and arenas.

Arena rock also refers to a musical style and genre in which artists create rock music designed for mainstream and commercial radio play. This includes highly-produced and performance-oriented songs, from power ballads to rock anthems.

Some critics assert that arena rock is more focused on broad audience appeal and showmanship based on visual aesthetics like fireworks rather than musical artistry. Despite this, arena rock and its performers have enjoyed success in touring and radio play.

As rock' n' roll expanded in the 1970s, technological advances in sound systems and special effects allowed bands to perform in even larger venues for massive crowds. To some degree, this focus on mainstream audiences led to a rise in punk rock and concentration on intimacy with listeners rather than excess. In addition, arena rock has evolved and influenced music in the decades following the 1970s, resulting in the widespread popularity of hair, glam, and pop-metal bands in the 1980s, such as Def Leppard, Bon Jovi, and Van Halen, and even post-grunge arena rock groups like Coldplay and Nickelback.

KISS formed in 1973 in New York City with band members Paul Stanley (vocals, guitar), Gene Simmons (vocals, bass guitar), Peter Criss (vocals, drums), and Ace Frehley (vocals, guitar.) In addition to intricate makeup and costumes, KISS brought the arena rock spectacle to a new level with pyrotechnics, fire-breathing, rockets, smoke, and blood-spitting.

In the latter half of the 1970s, KISS was one of the most commercially-successful rock bands, and its members had become pop culture icons. Though their popularity declined beginning in the 1980s, KISS is considered among the greatest metal and hard rock bands of all time and ranks on many lists in the top five best live bands of all time. The original members of KISS were inducted into the Rock & Roll Hall of Fame in 2014, and their influence continues today.

In addition to popularizing arena rock in the 1970s, Alice Cooper is considered the pioneer of "shock rock" due to his dark, theatrical performances. Alice Cooper was born Vincent Damon Furnier in 1948 and began his music career in 1964 in Arizona. In 1975, he legally changed his name to Alice Cooper and began his solo career with a concept album called *Welcome to My Nightmare*.

Alice Cooper is known for hard and glam rock, as well as heavy metal, new wave, and art rock. His performance style greatly influenced arena rock and heavy metal, combining horror elements with rock 'n' roll in legendary concerts and unforgettable showmanship.

[40]
THE CLASH:
PUNK ROCK REVOLUTION

The Clash formed in 1976 in London and became an integral part of the British punk rock revolution and international pop culture. Members included Joe Strummer (vocals, guitar), Mick Jones (guitar, vocals), Paul Simonon (bass), and Nicky Headon (drums). The Clash incorporated a variety of musical elements, including reggae, funk, dub, rockabilly, and hip-hop. Their experimentation and influence in the movements of punk rock, post-punk, new wave, and beyond echoes the phrase "The Only Band That Matters" — which is how they were billed.

The Clash released their first album, *The Clash*, in 1977, following up with *Give' Em Enough Rope* the following year, earning them commercial and critical success in the UK. Their third album, *London Calling*, became popular in the US as well and is considered one of the best albums of the 1980s. Their fifth album, *Combat Rock*, released in 1982, went double platinum in the US and featured the band's well-known hits "Rock the Casbah" and "Should I Stay or Should I Go."

Between 1982 and 1985, Headon and Jones both exited the group. With new members, The Clash recorded their last album, *Cut the Crap*, in 1985 before disbanding altogether.

The Clash was inducted into the Rock & Roll Hall of Fame in 2003, immediately following Joe Strummer's unexpected death. The band's legacy is not only as prolific creators and leaders of the punk music era but as symbols of artistic protest and rebellion against political and social issues such as racism, oppressive capitalism, and institutionalized violence. The Clash and their music remain important to rock history and culture today.

PART FIVE:
PUNK AND NEW WAVE
(LATE 1970s–EARLY 1980s)

Punk music emerged in the US and UK in the mid-1970s as a reaction to the mainstream rock 'n' roll of the time. It grew into an underground scene in highly urban cities, led by bands such as the Sex Pistols, The Clash, the Ramones, Blondie, and Iggy & the Stooges. This allowed for small, diverse, and local groups to develop their own sounds and subgenres that blended nonconformity, individuality, and a hard edge to music and performance.

Throughout the late 1970s and early 1980s, creators and fans of punk rock rejected industry pop music, cultural norms, and corporate capitalism, resulting in a fiercely independent mindset and do-it-yourself philosophy that influenced post-punk, new wave, and indie rock.

The subgenre of new wave represented a combination of such genres as punk, art rock, synth pop, and reggae. New wave bands emerged in the late 1970s in London and New York City and have had a big impact on pop rock.

Though punk and new wave overlap significantly, the use of synthesizers and electronic keyboards was a key element in the new wave movement, as was experimentation in rhythm. In addition, new wave music was far more prevalent within mainstream rock 'n' roll, especially with the advent of music videos and MTV.

[41]
THE RAMONES: GODFATHERS OF PUNK

The Ramones became the godfathers of punk rock through their style, attitudes, and sound in the 1970s. They defined this new genre, making them not only one of the most important bands in history but one that launched a revolution in the world of rock music. Like many bands, the Ramones experienced long-term tension among their members, but they continued to release albums and tour for nearly two decades.

Though the Ramones didn't enjoy the commercial success of many American contemporaries like Talking Heads and Blondie, they witnessed firsthand the explosion of punk rock in the UK out of musical roots they had established in New York City's club scene.

The band's original members met while attending Forest Hills High School in Queens, New York, with Joey on vocals, Johnny on guitar, Dee Dee as songwriter, and Tommy as drummer. Interestingly, none of the members were born with the last name Ramone, and their first names are stage names as well.

The group was influenced by several rock 'n' roll singer-songwriters, including Jimi Hendrix, the Beatles, the Stooges, and Led Zeppelin.

In 1974, the Ramones debuted at the club CBGB in New York City, quickly establishing themselves as a staple of the underground rock music scene. Their music was defined by Johnny's bare-essential guitar playing, Joey's memorable voice, and the band's uniquely straightforward stage presence.

The Ramones released their last album in 1995, playing their last show in Hollywood a year later. Bands such as Nirvana, Green Day, and Pearl Jam have acknowledged the Ramones' influence, and the band's resurgence of popularity in the 1990s demonstrated their importance to fans across decades.

Joey Ramone passed away in 2001, Dee Dee in 2002, Johnny in 2004, and Tommy in 2014. In 2002, the Ramones were inducted into the Rock & Roll Hall of Fame.

Though the original members are gone, the Ramones left a lasting imprint on punk rock. They embraced a style and sound separate from arena rock's complex performance artistry, inspiring young musicians by proving that, without a doubt, rock belongs to everyone.

[42]
SEX PISTOLS:
ANARCHY IN THE UK

The Sex Pistols formed in London in 1975 with initial members Johnny Rotten (vocalist), Steve Jones (guitarist), Paul Cook (drummer), and Glen Matlock (bassist), who was replaced by Sid Vicious in 1977. They're credited with beginning the punk movement in the UK.

Though the band was together for less than three years, the Sex Pistols were revolutionaries of punk rock and pop culture, inspiring generations of musicians and defining the image of punk.

They released their only studio album in 1977, *Never Mind the Bollocks, Here's the Sex Pistols*, which reached number one in the UK and is considered instrumental to the foundation of punk rock. The album ranks consistently among the lists of most important and greatest of all time.

During the last performance of their US tour in early 1978, Rotten announced the band's breakup. In 1979, Vicious died of a heroin overdose amid a scandal involving his arrest for the alleged murder of Nancy Spungen, his girlfriend. In the mid-1990s, the original members of the Sex Pistols reunited for a tour and have continued with independent performances.

The Sex Pistols were inducted into the Rock & Roll Hall of Fame in 2006, though they did not attend the ceremony. Many punk and post-punk bands directly credit the impact of the Sex Pistols on their music, including The Clash, Guns N' Roses, Nirvana, and Green Day. In addition, their punk fashion and rebellious image have become a symbol for generations of young people as an expression of radicalism and disaffection with society. From the performance of their single "God Save the Queen" on the Thames to their infamous concert at Manchester's Lesser Free Trade Hall, the Sex Pistols will remain legends in rock 'n' roll history.

[43]
BLONDIE:
PUNK GOES POP

Blondie was formed by singer Deborah Harry and guitarist Chris Stein in 1974 in New York City. The group was a significant part of the punk and new wave movement, as well as the underground NYC music scene in the mid-1970s. After achieving success in the UK and Australian music markets, Blondie received critical acclaim in the US with their third album, *Parallel Lines*, in 1978. The band is known for many number-one singles, including "Heart of Glass," "Call Me," "The Tide Is High," and "Rapture," all of which brought them fame outside the punk scene in the world of popular music.

Not only was Blondie known for their varied musical style, which included punk, disco, reggae, funk, and pop, but Deborah Harry became an inspiration as the lead singer and frontwoman of an all-male band in what was definitely a male-dominated culture at the time. Female artists such as Madonna and Lady Gaga recognize Harry for her pioneering path and influence. In addition, though certainly not the first rap song to be produced and released, Blondie's "Rapture" is considered the first rap single to top the US charts. When it was released in 1981, rap and hip-hop were fairly unknown to mainstream American listeners, but Blondie's hit helped bring rap and hip-hop to a larger audience.

After releasing their sixth studio album in 1982, Blondie disbanded. Stein was diagnosed with a rare autoimmune skin disease, and Harry took time to care for him and pursue a solo career. Blondie reunited in 1997 and continues to perform. In 2006, they were inducted into the Rock & Roll Hall of Fame.

[44]
TALKING HEADS: ART PUNK INNOVATORS

In 1975, Talking Heads initially appeared on the New York City punk scene as a supporting act for the Ramones at CBGB. Band members included frontman David Byrne (vocals, guitar), Tina Weymouth (bass), Chris Frantz (drums), and Jerry Harrison (guitar, keyboards). With their combination of punk, funk, art rock, and international cultural music elements, Talking Heads had become one of the most innovative and artistic bands of the post-punk and new wave movements by the 1980s.

Byrne and Frantz, members of a band called the Artistics, met Weymouth at the Rhode Island School of Design, with Harrison joining later in New York. In 1977, Talking Heads released their debut album, *Talking Heads: 77*, to positive reviews. The group collaborated with a variety of artists and musicians, and in 1983, they achieved widespread popularity with the single "Burning Down the House." Their bestselling album *Little Creatures* was released in 1985. In 1991, Talking Heads disbanded, with Byrne pursuing a solo career and the other members continuing to perform as well.

Talking Heads is considered one of the greatest and most influential bands of all time, with legendary hits such as "Once in a Lifetime," "Psycho Killer," and "Life During Wartime," which was named in 2020 among the "500 Songs That Shaped Rock" by James Henke, the chief curator for the Rock & Roll Hall of Fame at the time. The band was inducted into the Rock & Roll Hall of Fame in 2002.

A variety of musicians have cited the Talking Heads' influence on their music, including Vampire Weekend, Trent Reznor, Kesha, St. Vincent, and Eddie Vedder. Radiohead got their band name from the 1986 song "Radio Head" by Talking Heads, and Jonathan Demme's *Stop Making Sense* is considered one of the best concert films ever made—showcasing the brilliance of the band's live performances and artistic style across three nights of Talking Heads concerts in Hollywood in 1983.

[45]
THE POLICE:
REGGAE-ROCK FUSION

In 1977, The Police formed in London with frontman Sting (singer/songwriter, bass guitarist), Andy Summers (guitarist), and Stewart Copeland (drummer). The trio became internationally known in the late 1970s, gaining worldwide popularity with their musical fusion of rock, reggae, punk, and more.

Though The Police were together for less than a decade, they had a huge impact on British new wave music, as well as pop culture. Considered by many as a punk band when they started, The Police included reggae, new wave, jazz, progressive rock, and pop elements in their music.

Their debut album, *Outlandos d'Amour*, received attention for the singles "Roxanne" and "Can't Stand Losing You." The band's subsequent albums, released in 1979, 1980, and 1981, garnered The Police commercial and critical success with songs such as "Message in a Bottle," "Don't Stand So Close to Me," and "Every Little Thing She Does Is Magic."

Sting's previous career as a high school English teacher influenced his narrative lyrics and literary references, which—combined with the varied backgrounds and elevated instrumentation of Copeland and Summers—created a unique blend of musical genres. The band's ambitious sound and lyrics, in addition to their unique world touring locations, allowed them to incorporate political ideals and international cultural elements into their music.

Synchronicity, released in 1983, was the last studio album recorded by The Police and their most successful, with the lead single "Every Breath You Take." The group formally disbanded in 1986, though the members reunited in 2007 for the highest-grossing tour of that year.

The Police are one of the bestselling bands in rock 'n' roll history and earned six Grammys. They were inducted into the Rock & Roll Hall of Fame in 2003, and their albums are consistently mentioned on greatest-of-all-time lists.

Sting has continued his success with a solo career, as have Summers and Copeland. The Police will long be remembered as part of the punk and new wave movement with global mainstream popularity due to their unique blend of sound and sophisticated lyrics.

[46]
ICONIC PERFORMANCE: THE SEX PISTOLS ON THE THAMES

In 1977, Queen Elizabeth II celebrated her 25th year as the British monarch with a Silver Jubilee, which included a procession down the Thames scheduled for June 9th of that year. Malcolm McLaren, manager of the Sex Pistols at the time, had the band sail down the Thames on June 7, 1977, two days before the queen's scheduled river procession, in order to perform their subversive single, "God Save the Queen," whose lyrics expressed a controversial take on the monarchy.

When the boat docked, a scuffle broke out with the police, and Malcolm McLaren, Johnny Rotten, and several other band members were arrested. Though the performance was intended as a parody, it offended many people in Britain and around the world. However, record sales for the band skyrocketed.

Overall, the Sex Pistols on the Thames became a symbol of punk music's youthful culture and anarchist style that spread across England and inspired other bands in the genre, including The Clash.

[47]
LANDMARK ALBUM:
THE RAMONES' *RAMONES*

The Ramones' first album, *Ramones*, was released by Sire Records in April 1976. Though well-reviewed by critics, it did not achieve commercial success. The singles "Blitzkrieg Bop" and "I Wanna Be Your Boyfriend" didn't make the charts either, though they're well-known today. The album reflected the band's range with their dark, sometimes humorous, lyrics and their bare-bones instrumentation.

Like many landmark albums, the cover of *Ramones* has an interesting story behind it. It features a black-and-white photograph of the Ramones wearing leather jackets and faded jeans and standing against a brick wall, a setup that other bands have widely imitated for their album covers. However, the photo, which was originally intended to accompany a story in the fanzine *Punk*, was used only because the record label rejected the initial cover art.

Today, *Ramones* is considered one of the most impactful and classic punk rock albums. Its influence extends to grunge and heavy metal as well, inspiring bands from The Clash and Green Day to Metallica and Red Hot Chili Peppers. Though the album did not enjoy mainstream popularity at the time of its release, there's no question as to its longevity and increasing appreciation with each decade.

[48]
THE RISE OF INDIE LABELS: SST, SUB POP, AND MORE

The punk and new wave movements of the late 1970s and early 1980s led to a rise in "indie," or independent, record labels. This was a significant development in rock 'n' roll, as major corporate labels have historically held artists to strict contractual obligations that not only call into question artist rights of ownership but also manufactured messaging and engineered popularity among fans.

Indie labels are known for being more progressive and artist-centric in terms of creative control, smaller rosters, and valuing integrity over profit. They're also important to rock 'n' roll culture in their discovery and promotion of bands and artists outside the mainstream.

Rock music began with independent labels like Sun Records and Chess Records. However, the emergence of punk and new wave artists and their DIY culture allowed indie labels to grow and succeed so artists could release their music independent of big corporate influence and restriction.

Labels such as SST, Sub Pop, Alternative Tentacles, and Homestead Records were based around the country, from Long Beach and San Francisco, California, to Seattle to New York's Long Island. Access to the production, distribution, and support of labels outside the mainstream, though lower than corporate labels, allowed fans to discover new and diverse music and artists to embrace a sense of authenticity and independence.

[49]
THE NEW WAVE SOUND: DEVO AND THE B-52'S

Devo and the B-52's helped define the new wave movement that began in the late 1970s continuing into the 1980s. Both bands contributed to new wave through their use of instruments, technology, and even fashion to establish rock personas. The bands' origins epitomized the punk and post-punk DIY ethos, with roots in college settings and early performances in small venues that drew a loyal cult following. Later, Devo and the B-52's earned legendary fans, including David Bowie, Iggy Pop, David Byrne, and even John Lennon.

Devo formed in Akron, Ohio, in 1973. Members included brothers Mark and Bob Mothersbaugh, Gerald and Bob Casale, and Alan Myers. The band's name comes from the social concept of "de-evolution"—the regression of humans and society. This idea infused their music and lyrics with elements of irony, satire, and surrealism, as well as bleak political commentary.

Devo's early work featured experimental electronics and dissonant rock, reflecting their art-punk background. In the 1980s, Devo was known for synth pop new wave and a style of performance art that often included their now-iconic yellow jumpsuits and red "flowerpot" hats.

In 2019, Devo was nominated for induction into the Rock & Roll Hall of Fame. Though many would consider the group to be a one-hit wonder, with 1980's "Whip It" as their only commercially-successful song, Devo's music had a definite impact on new wave, as well as alternative rock.

The B-52's formed in 1976 in Athens, Georgia. Members included Kate Pierson, Fred Schneider, Ricky Wilson, Cindy Wilson, and Keith Strickland. They played shows at CBGB and Max's Kansas

City in New York City before the release of their first single, "Rock Lobster," in 1978.

Their innovative sound, abstract lyrics, and quirky style made them an important part of the emergence of new wave and underground post-punk, along with bands like Talking Heads and Blondie.

The B-52's popularized a campy aesthetic and liberated performance style that reinforced individuality, inclusion, and acceptance through new wave rock 'n' roll. This is especially evident in the commercial and critical success of their 1989 album, *Cosmic Thing*, including hits such as "Roam" and "Love Shack."

Unlike many of their contemporaries, the B-52's embraced an apolitical approach and positive tone, which reinforced their DIY roots, experimental identity, and welcome of outsiders to the mainstream.

[50]
PUNK'S DIY ETHIC: FANZINES AND INDEPENDENT GIGS

One aspect that sets punk apart from other rock music genres is the DIY ethic of its underground subculture. In a sense, this mindset derived out of necessity, as many counterculture movements are.

Historically, the punk music scene was outside mainstream rock 'n' roll, giving marginalized communities of LGBTQ+, women, and BIPOC (Black, Indigenous, People of Color) participants an opportunity to create, collaborate, and perform. Though economically and commercially challenging, this also allowed artists to organize independently, giving them the ability to focus attention on issues of social justice in self-organized gigs, self-produced records, and "fanzines."

Fanzines surfaced in the US and UK as punk counterculture's response to traditional print media. In 1976, *Punk* emerged in New York City, and other influential fanzines popped up in regional areas from Los Angeles and Washington, DC, to London. These publications facilitated the growth, popularity, and success of punk and alternative rock through the 1980s and into the 1990s.

Generally, fanzines are DIY, local, and unofficial, with contributions from unpaid writers, illustrators, and editors. They're circulated and enjoyed by enthusiasts and had a large impact on punk music and culture, as they were predominantly produced by fans rather than professionals.

Fanzines were also instrumental in promoting independent gigs and performances put on by punk bands and artists, often with support from underground clubs like New York's CBGB and London's Roxy in the 1970s and '80s.

The DIY ethic of punk music and culture has not only provided a foundation of connection and exposure for the genre's fans and artists, but it also gave many marginalized groups and individuals of all identities a voice and representation outside of mainstream rock 'n' roll.

Of course, there are still issues in terms of acceptance for some, besides basic commercialism restraints, such as the closing of venues. Yet the punk community epitomizes creating space for collaboration, inclusivity, and artistic independence, unlike many other rock subgenres.

PART SIX:
THE 1980S ROCK SCENE

The 1980s transformed the rock scene from traditional rock 'n' roll to new wave and synthesized pop. The decade produced global superstars such as Michael Jackson, Duran Duran, Prince, Cyndi Lauper, Whitney Houston, and Madonna, as well as genres such as dance, synth pop, glam metal, and indie music. Musicians of the 1980s continued to push boundaries, using music as a platform for self-expression and sociopolitical commentary.

Digital synthesizers, drum machines, and other technological innovations provided new electronic sounds, changing the way music was recorded, edited, and produced. In addition, the advent of MTV and music videos broke ground for artists and fans, intertwining visual style and musical expression.

This manifested in youth subcultures of punk, new wave, gothic rock, and hip-hop. The diversity and variety of the 1980s rock scene provided something for everyone, and nostalgia for this decade continues in modern media and trends.

[51]
AC/DC:
HIGH-VOLTAGE ROCK

AC/DC was formed in 1973 in Sydney, Australia, by guitarist brothers Angus and Malcolm Young. The band gained initial success in Australia and Europe in the mid-1970s, but their breakout album in the US was 1979's *Highway to Hell*. Unfortunately, lead vocalist Bon Scott died of alcohol poisoning just seven months after the album's release. Though the other members of AC/DC thought of disbanding after Scott's death, they welcomed Brian Johnson from the UK as a new frontman for the group and dedicated 1980's *Back in Black* to Bon Scott.

Back in Black is not only one of the bestselling albums of all time but is considered by many music historians and critics to be one of the greatest rock 'n' roll albums in history.

In 1981, AC/DC released another successful album, *For Those About to Rock*, but the remainder of the decade saw a great deal of turnover for the band members. Despite the many challenges the band faced, their music symbolizes what many fans feel is the very heart of rock 'n' roll, and their legacy continues.

AC/DC was inducted into the Rock & Roll Hall of Fame in 2003. Their blend of hard rock and heavy metal remains influential today, as do their high-energy performance level and iconic guitar riffs, which inspired bands from Metallica to Guns N' Roses. In addition, AC/DC's cultural impact has spread through the use of their music in movies, video games, television, and stadium sporting events.

[52]
GUNS N' ROSES:
THE MOST DANGEROUS BAND

In 1985, two local bands—Hollywood Rose and L.A. Guns—merged to form Guns N' Roses in Los Angeles, California. The group, which included Axl Rose (vocalist), Slash (guitarist), Duff McKagan (bassist), Izzy Stradlin (guitarist), and Steven Adler (drummer), scored a contract with Geffen Records a year later. Today, additional members include Richard Fortus, Frank Ferrer, Dizzy Reed, and Melissa Reese.

The band became known in West Coast clubs for their live performances and unique sound, influenced by metal, punk, blues, and classic rock. In 1987, Guns N' Roses released their first album, *Appetite for Destruction*. Though it took a while to gain mainstream popularity, it became one of the bestselling albums of all time, with hit songs like "Welcome to the Jungle" and "Sweet Child O' Mine."

On top of Axl Rose's unpredictability, the band gained a reputation for controversy and partying and was labeled the "most dangerous band in the world." They struggled with lawsuits, drug and alcohol issues, feuds with other bands, and even concert riots.

Nevertheless, Guns N' Roses continued to produce iconic albums, songs, and music videos until the early 1990s, including memorable covers of "Knockin' on Heaven's Door" and "Live and Let Die." They served as an alternative to glam metal rock in the 1980s with their unique hard rock and heavy metal sound and innovative rock ballads.

Guns N' Roses was inducted into the Rock & Roll Hall of Fame in 2012, and many of the band's members have established themselves as legendary artists and musicians in their own right. They held some of the greatest influence in rock music from the mid-1980s to the early 1990s, and several of their classic songs and videos are still considered groundbreaking today.

Guns N' Roses has inspired bands like Nirvana, Soundgarden, and Alice in Chains, and their legacy will remain as one of the bestselling, impactful, and notorious bands in rock history.

[53]
BON JOVI:
HAIR METAL HEROES

The band Bon Jovi formed in 1983 in New Jersey and became a symbol of hair metal with their aesthetic and musical blend of heavy metal, pop, and rock. Original members still with the band include frontman Jon Bon Jovi, Tico Torres (drummer), David Bryan (keyboard), Phil X, and Hugh McDonald. John Shanks, Everett Bradley, Alec John Such, and Richie Sambora have also joined the group at one time or another.

Bon Jovi enjoyed commercial success with their first two albums but achieved a global audience in 1986 with their third album, *Slippery When Wet*, featuring the iconic hits "You Give Love a Bad Name" and "Livin' on a Prayer."

Bon Jovi continued to be one of the most successful bands in rock' n' roll throughout the 1980s and beyond, with top hits including "Bad Medicine," millions of record sales, and legendary tours. Their innovative rock anthems, power ballads, and relatable lyrics have influenced bands from Skid Row to Daughtry. In addition, Bon Jovi's less-controversial offstage reputation made the group more palatable to mainstream audiences.

One of the bestselling US rock bands in history, Bon Jovi was inducted into the Rock & Roll Hall of Fame in 2018. Besides Jon Bon Jovi's legacy as the band's talented and influential frontman, he's also well-known for his charitable foundation and its humanitarian efforts to address hunger, poverty, and homelessness, as well as numerous innovative programs to benefit communities and veterans. Through philanthropy and the joy brought to fans for over four decades, Bon Jovi is certainly a hair metal hero.

[54]
METALLICA:
THRASH METAL TITANS

Thrash metal emerged with bands such as Metallica, Slayer, Anthrax, and Megadeth in the early 1980s as an extreme version of heavy metal. Aggressive tempo and complex guitar riffs characterized the subgenre. Thrash metal was a reaction to conservatism and more moderate forms of metal that were popular at the time.

Metallica was a leader of the thrash metal movement in the US, formed in 1981 by James Hetfield (vocals, guitar) and Lars Ulrich (drums) in Los Angeles. Current members include Kirk Hammett (guitar) and Robert Trujillo (bass). Dave Mustaine, a former member of Metallica, formed Megadeth when he left the group.

Black Sabbath's dark and heavy sound had a significant impact on Metallica's founding members. Their third album, *Master of*

Puppets, was released in 1986 and is considered one of the band's greatest and most commercially-successful recordings. In 1988, Metallica was nominated for their first Grammy with the album *...And Justice for All.*

In the 1990s, the band deviated from thrash metal toward a more mainstream sound. However, in 2008, Metallica's ninth album returned to thrash metal once again. In addition to being known as thrash metal titans, Metallica was also involved in the copyright case against Napster in 1999.

Nearly a decade later, in 2009, the band was inducted into the Rock & Roll Hall of Fame. Throughout their career, Metallica has won 10 Grammys and sold over 125 million albums worldwide, earning them a place among the most commercially-successful and greatest rock bands of all time. Metallica paved the way for numerous future musicians, influencing the heavy and thrash metal genres and achieving unprecedented mainstream success.

[55]
U2:
THE IRISH SUPERSTARS

U2 formed in Dublin, Ireland, in 1976. Members, including frontman Bono (vocals, rhythm guitar), the Edge (lead guitar, keyboards), Larry Mullen Jr. (drums), and Adam Clayton (bass guitar) met as teenagers in school. They released their first album, *Boy*, in 1980.

By the mid-1980s, U2 was known for hits such as "Sunday Bloody Sunday" and "Pride (In the Name of Love)" and incredible live performances, including an appearance at Live Aid in 1985. For decades, the group has influenced music and pop culture with their artistic style, meaningful lyrics, and political and social activism.

In 1987, the band's fifth album, *The Joshua Tree*, became their bestselling and most critically-acclaimed record, with hits such as "With or Without You" and "I Still Haven't Found What I'm Looking For." They followed up with a double album, *Rattle and Hum*, in 1988.

U2's music incorporates classic and alternative rock with experimental elements of electronic dance and industrial music. Their humanitarian efforts across the globe have aided many groups and individuals in need, shedding light on important causes, from human rights to poverty, creating as much an impact in philanthropy as rock 'n' roll.

U2 has won 22 Grammys over the course of their career — in addition to numerous other awards — and they were inducted into the Rock & Roll Hall of Fame in 2005. They're consistently ranked among the greatest and bestselling artists of all time. Their legendary concerts have continuously sold out, earning them second place as one of the highest-grossing musical acts across four decades.

In 2022, U2 became the fifth musical group to receive Kennedy Center Honors for contributions to the performing arts. In addition, U2 was the first band to perform at the Sphere Las Vegas, with a 40-concert residency of "U2: UV Achtung Baby Live" beginning in September 2023 and ending in March 2024.

[56]
DEF LEPPARD: PYROMANIA AND BEYOND

In 1976, Def Leppard formed in Sheffield, England. The band's primary members since 1992 include Joe Elliott (vocals), Rick Savage (bass), Rick Allen (drums), Vivian Campbell (guitar and vocals), and Phil Collen (guitar and vocals.) Def Leppard achieved widespread popularity as part of the British heavy metal wave of the 1980s and continues to make music and tour today.

Many fans consider Def Leppard among the greatest live performers and innovators, combining spectacular visual and sonic elements. This includes the pioneering use of screen images, lighting, and lasers.

One of the band's most memorable performances, and a landmark in rock history as well, was the 1986 onstage comeback of Def Leppard's drummer, Rick Allen, whose left arm had been severed in a car accident on New Year's Eve 1984. The performance marked Allen's recovery and mastery of the ability to drum with one arm—less than two years after the accident.

In 2019, Def Leppard was inducted into the Rock & Roll Hall of Fame, reflecting their decades-long contribution to rock music, from iconic albums to influential performances. Their albums *Pyromania* (1983) and *Hysteria* (1987) are multiplatinum bestsellers, featuring hit singles such as "Pour Some Sugar on Me," "Love Bites," and "Rock of Ages."

Not only is Def Leppard consistently ranked as one of the greatest rock artists, but they're also one of only five groups with two original studio albums that sell more than 10 million copies in the US.

[57]
ICONIC PERFORMANCE: U2 AT LIVE AID

U2 was among the many musical acts at Live Aid in July 1985. Though they hadn't attained rock stardom just yet, the Irish band's performance at Wembley Stadium in support of famine relief for Ethiopia became iconic—second only, perhaps, to that of Freddie Mercury and Queen. In fact, music historians have pointed to Live Aid as the launching-off point for U2 and frontman Bono's rock 'n' roll success, demonstrating their legendary showmanship and talent onstage to wide audience appeal.

U2 began their performance with "Sunday Bloody Sunday," followed by "Bad." During "Bad," Bono reportedly noticed a young woman in the audience being crushed against the security barrier by the crowds. He tried to communicate the problem to security, but when that didn't work, Bono stepped off the stage to help pull her away from the crowd and ended up dancing with her while his bandmates continued to play.

Due to the unforeseen circumstances that extended the song "Bad" to about 12 minutes, U2 was unable to play the third song they had lined up: "Pride (In the Name of Love)." Decades later, Kal Khalique, the young woman in the audience, stated that Bono had saved her life during that iconic performance at Live Aid.

[58]
LANDMARK ALBUM:
METALLICA'S *MASTER OF PUPPETS*

Metallica released their third studio album, *Master of Puppets*, in March 1986. It received critical acclaim, was a huge commercial success, and is still considered one of the most impactful metal albums ever. Though there were no music videos released and almost no radio play, *Master of Puppets* sold over half a million copies in its first year and became the first platinum album in the thrash metal genre.

Metallica's landmark album is known for its heavy themes and socially-conscious lyrics about power, oppression, and alienation. Cliff Burton, the band's bassist, composed and arranged many of the songs; unfortunately, during the band's tour in Sweden, Burton died in a bus accident.

Despite this tragedy, 1986 marked an influential year for metal, as thrash metal emerged from the underground scene with albums by Megadeth, Slayer, and Anthrax. However, it is *Master of Puppets* that solidified Metallica's importance as a band and creative force among both metal and mainstream artists.

In 2015, the Library of Congress chose *Master of Puppets* to be preserved in the National Recording Registry — the first metal recording to have that honor.

Many rock 'n' roll historians, in and out of the metal genre, maintain that Metallica redefined heavy metal with their lyrics and sound. Meanwhile, *Master of Puppets* continually appears in mainstream media as well as on *Thrash Metal Magazine's* "Best Albums" lists decades after its release.

[59]
THE GLAM METAL ERA: MÖTLEY CRÜE AND POISON

Glam metal was definitely a huge part of rock 'n' roll in the 1980s. In terms of style, glam metal blends traditional heavy metal with hard and punk rock, combined with pop elements. Glam metal bands often incorporated "shred" guitar solos in their songs and wrote power ballads that appealed to mainstream listeners.

It's not just about sound, though — glam metal's aesthetic derives from 1970s glam rock: lots of hairspray, makeup, tight clothing, and a reputation for partying and scandal. Mötley Crüe and Poison are two of the most well-known and influential glam metal bands.

Mötley Crüe was formed by Nikki Sixx (bassist) and Tommy Lee (drummer) in 1981 in Hollywood, California. Mick Mars (guitarist) and Vince Neil (vocalist) joined the band soon after. Their third album, *Theatre of Pain*, was released in 1985 and marked Mötley Crüe's transition from heavy metal to glam metal.

Their live performances epitomized the glam metal style, using pyrotechnics, androgynous costumes, and even lighting Nikki Sixx on fire.

Mötley Crüe developed a reputation for a wild offstage lifestyle, becoming notorious for trashing hotel rooms, partying with groupies, and abusing alcohol and drugs. Their iconic performances, metal sound, and rebellious image made Mötley Crüe legendary in the world of glam metal.

Formed in 1983 in Pennsylvania, Poison was another groundbreaking glam metal band. The group's most well-known members include frontman Bret Michaels, Rikki Rockett (drums), C.C. DeVille (guitar), and Bobby Dall (bass.)

Poison enjoyed huge commercial success in the mid-to-late 1980s, with their number-one song "Every Rose Has Its Thorn" and millions of records sold. Among the band's multiplatinum albums are their 1986 debut, *Look What the Cat Dragged In*, followed by *Open Up* and *Say… Ahh!*, and *Flesh & Blood*. True to the genre, Poison also gained a reputation for their live performances and offstage partying.

[60]
THE EVOLUTION OF HEAVY METAL: IRON MAIDEN AND JUDAS PRIEST

Heavy metal underwent an evolutionary movement starting in England in the 1970s but spread internationally in the early 1980s. Many music historians refer to this phenomenon as the new wave of British heavy metal, or NWOBHM—a primarily blue-collar movement reacting to the 1960s counterculture and 1970s over-the-top arena rock.

In many ways, NWOBHM was a fusion of classic heavy metal and punk rock elements, including underground beginnings, DIY attitudes, and a sense of bleak isolation in reaction to mainstream society. As a result, a heavy metal subculture took root, spreading from the UK to the US and beyond. Two of the most influential and successful bands of the NWOBHM were Iron Maiden and Judas Priest.

In 1975, songwriter and bassist Steve Harris formed Iron Maiden just outside of London. Other primary members of this heavy metal group include Bruce Dickinson (vocals), Nicko McBrain (drums), Dave Murray, Adrian Smith, and Janick Gers — all guitarists.

In the 1980s, Iron Maiden pioneered the new wave of British heavy metal, most notably with the 1982 release of *The Number of the Beast* — considered among the best heavy metal albums of all time — with 41 albums to their name and thousands of live shows. The group has won Grammys and BRIT Awards and received nominations for the Rock & Roll Hall of Fame.

In addition to their NWOBHM influence and mainstream popularity, Iron Maiden is known for their intellectual impact on heavy metal culture through historical and poetic references in their lyrics.

Known as pioneers of NWOBHM, Judas Priest formed in England in 1969 and are credited with helping to develop other subgenres like speed, thrash, and power metal, as well. Judas Priest didn't gain much commercial success until the release of their sixth studio album, *British Steel*, in 1980. With this mainstream traction, Judas Priest attained success in the worlds of glam and heavy metal.

The group's wardrobe — leather and spikes — became iconic, as did their vocal and guitar sounds. Though the band has seen a high turnover in terms of members, Judas Priest was inducted into the Rock & Roll Hall of Fame in 2022 with the Award for Musical Excellence, reflecting their unique contribution to the evolution of heavy metal in the 1980s and musical influence spanning decades.

PART SEVEN:
THE RISE OF ALTERNATIVE
ROCK (1990S)

The rise of alternative rock in the 1990s indicated an important movement in American culture and its music industry. Like the counterculture of the 1960s, alternative rock was a response to popular mainstream rock—and what appeared to many disillusioned young people as superficial, manufactured conformity.

Grunge, a subgenre of alternative rock associated with Seattle, was influenced by hardcore punk and heavy metal, resulting in darker and grittier music and producing a more dissonant and distorted sound. This stood in contrast to the more "professional" and stylized aesthetic of mainstream rock predominant in the 1980s.

The lyrics associated with much of 1990s alternative in America also reflect themes of social consciousness and a sense of isolation and self-doubt.

As the alternative rock movement took hold in the US, Britpop (British pop music) emerged in contrast as a musical and societal revolution. This 1990s British rock style featured more melodic songs and lyrics than American grunge, containing unique references to British life and the culture of the working class.

Britpop reflected the UK's musical heritage of 1960s rock, the indie rock movement of the 1980s, and some punk as well. Ultimately, Britpop was also a call to action for authenticity and individuality in music.

[61]
NIRVANA: GRUNGE EXPLOSION

In the early 1990s, Nirvana generated a "grunge" music explosion that appealed to a disillusioned youth culture, changing rock 'n' roll history. The band was formed in 1987 in Aberdeen, Washington, by Kurt Cobain (lead vocals, guitar) and Krist

Novoselic (bass). In 1990, Dave Grohl joined as the band's drummer. Nirvana became part of the early Seattle grunge scene and released their debut album, *Bleach with Sub Pop,* in 1989. It gained traction among mainstream listeners with its hit single "Smells Like Teen Spirit" from 1991's *Nevermind.*

Nirvana's music and grunge aesthetic became integral to pop culture, making them one of the most successful alternative rock bands in history. Their unique sound and musical themes of social alienation appealed to listeners around the world.

In 1993, the band's third album, *In Utero,* was a commercial and critical success. Unfortunately, Cobain's suicide in April 1994 caused Nirvana to disband. The live album of their performance for *MTV Unplugged* in New York was released in 1994.

Though Nirvana's career only lasted for a short time, their influence on rock 'n' roll continues to be felt among fellow musicians and new generations of fans. In addition to millions of albums sold, the band earned several awards—including a Grammy.

In 2014, Nirvana was inducted into the Rock & Roll Hall of Fame in their first year of eligibility. They consistently make all-time-greatest lists for inspiring and defining alternative rock.

[62]
PEARL JAM:
THE CONSCIOUS ROCKERS

Pearl Jam formed in 1990 in Seattle, Washington. Founding members include frontman Eddie Vedder (vocals, guitar), Jeff Ament (bass guitar), Mike McCready (lead guitar), Stone Gossard (rhythm guitar), and Matt Cameron (drums) as of 1998. The band's debut, *Ten,* achieved worldwide popularity and is one of the highest-selling albums of all time, followed by 1993's *Vs.* and 1994's *Vitalogy,* which were both record-setting successes.

Pearl Jam is associated with pioneering the grunge movement, but they've continued to be one of the most important influences on rock beyond the Seattle music scene of the 1990s.

Pearl Jam is also known for their conscientious approach to making music and defiance of the commercialization of the music industry. The group boycotted and sued Ticketmaster for its monopolization of concert sales and the resulting negative effects on both musicians and fans.

Pearl Jam unequivocally impacted pop culture through political and social activism, using their influence to address causes such as homelessness, environmentalism, and women's and veterans' rights.

In 2017, Pearl Jam was inducted into the Rock & Roll Hall of Fame. Their catalog of music extends beyond the grunge genre, and songs such as "Black" and "Jeremy" have contributed to important issues like inequality and suicide prevention. Pearl Jam's commitment to philanthropy and social advocacy—not to mention their artistic talent and authenticity—have made the band rock legends and a voice for multiple generations.

[63]
RADIOHEAD: EXPERIMENTAL INNOVATORS

Though Radiohead formed in Oxfordshire, England, in 1985, their influence during the rise of 1990s alternative rock is nearly unparalleled. Members of the band include Thom Yorke (vocals, guitar, piano), Colin Greenwood (bass) and brother Jonny (guitar, keyboard), Ed O'Brien (guitar), and Philip Selway (drums).

Radiohead released their first album in 1993, and their debut single, "Creep," brought them international popularity. 1995's *The Bends* received critical acclaim, but it was their third album,

1997's *OK Computer*, that established Radiohead as legends in alternative rock.

In addition to Radiohead's innovative music, they utilized a combination of artistic videos, live performances, and thought-provoking lyrics to deliver political and societal messages on everything from environmentalism and technology to social alienation. This had a large impact on bands such as Muse, Coldplay, and the Killers.

Radiohead continued to release albums with experimental styles and topical lyrics into the 2000s. The band has won six Grammys and is counted among the greatest rock 'n' roll artists of all time, with an induction into the Rock & Roll Hall of Fame in 2019.

Radiohead not only revolutionized rock music in the 1990s by pushing boundaries with electronic, classical, and jazz elements, but it also deeply influenced alternative culture.

[64]
RED HOT CHILI PEPPERS: FUNK-ROCK FUSION

The Red Hot Chili Peppers formed in 1982 in Los Angeles with members Anthony Kiedis (vocals), Flea (bass), Chad Smith (drums), and John Frusciante (guitar). Hillel Slovak and Jack Irons were part of the band until 1988.

The band is known for eclectic, genre-transcending music that embraces funk, punk, hard rock, metal, hip-hop, psychedelic rock, and alternative rock elements.

In 1991, the album *Blood Sugar Sex Magik* received critical and commercial success with hits such as "Under the Bridge" and "Give It Away." This led to huge popularity for the Red Hot Chili Peppers and is considered a groundbreaking album in alternative rock.

Guitarist Dave Navarro replaced Frusciante from 1992 to 1998. Frusciante rejoined Red Hot Chili Peppers after Navarro exited, and in 1999, the band released their most commercially-successful album, *Californication*. Unfortunately, the band was affected in the 1990s by struggles with drug use and addiction among some members, though they continued to record and perform and continue touring today.

The Red Hot Chili Peppers set several records on the Billboard Alternative Songs chart, including most number-one singles, cumulative weeks at number one, and top ten songs. They won three Grammys and were inducted into the Rock & Roll Hall of Fame in 2012 (minus guitarists Jack Sherman and Dave Navarro).

The Red Hot Chili Peppers have influenced bands such as Limp Bizkit, Smashing Pumpkins, Linkin Park, Maroon 5, and Logic. Their fusion of funk, alternative, metal, psychedelic, punk, and hard rock formed a legacy of innovation and rock' n' roll artistry.

[65]
OASIS:
BRITPOP KINGS

Oasis formed in Manchester, England, in 1991 with vocalist Liam Gallagher, guitarist Paul Arthurs, bass guitarist Paul McGuigan, and drummer Tony McCarroll. Liam Gallagher invited his older brother and guitarist/vocalist Noel to join, and Noel eventually became the band's songwriter as well. With accessible pop and lyrics containing British references, Oasis is considered a pioneer of the Britpop movement of the 1990s.

Oasis's debut album, *Definitely Maybe*, was released in 1994, setting numerous records, including the fastest-selling debut album in Britain at the time. Their 1995 album, *(What's the Story) Morning Glory?*, was a huge success in the UK and internationally and became one of the bestselling albums of all time. This was especially significant for Oasis in their publicly-inflated rivalry with fellow Britpop band Blur.

In 1996, Oasis set the record at that time for the biggest outdoor concerts in Britain with their two performances at Knebworth. However, the Gallagher brothers earned a reputation for public disputes and a somewhat reckless lifestyle in the latter half of the 1990s. This, along with other issues, led to heavy turnover among band members.

Though Oasis released studio albums between 2000 and 2008, Noel Gallagher's departure in 2009 led the group to disband. Despite this, Liam and Noel Gallagher went on to have solo careers.

Ultimately, Oasis is one of the most commercially-successful bands of all time — and not just among Britpop fans. Their albums have won numerous awards, and their singles have topped international charts, solidifying their contribution to alternative rock and lasting influence on rock 'n' roll.

[66]
GREEN DAY:
POP PUNK REVOLUTION

In 1987, Billie Joe Armstrong (lead vocals, guitar) and Mike Dirnt (bass, vocals) formed the band that would eventually become Green Day in Rodeo, California. Tré Cool (drums) joined in 1990. Green Day was part of the Berkeley/Bay Area punk scene, and their debut album, *Dookie*, achieved international success, in addition to bringing early 1990s punk rock to mainstream America with hits such as "Longview" and "When I Come Around."

Green Day's seventh album, *American Idiot*, was released in 2004. It was adapted in 2010 as a Broadway musical, which was nominated for Best Musical at the Tony Awards and won for best scenic and lighting designs. *American Idiot* reflects the band's political activism and criticism of America's hard-right politicians and conservative media, a stance their music and performances continue to reflect today.

In 2015, their first year of eligibility, Green Day was inducted into the Rock & Roll Hall of Fame. The band has won five Grammys and is one of the bestselling groups of all time. *Dookie* is consistently rated as an important album in the pop punk, punk, and alternative genres and earned a spot on the Rock & Roll Hall of Fame's list of 200 Classic Albums.

Green Day will continue to be known as one of the best punk rock bands in history, influencing generations of artists, including Fall Out Boy, Avril Lavigne, Lady Gaga, Blink-182, and Billie Eilish.

[67]
ICONIC PERFORMANCE: NIRVANA UNPLUGGED

MTV Unplugged was a popular television series in the 1990s that showcased musicians and bands in an acoustic setting, performing their hits with minimal instrumentation. Though asked repeatedly, Nirvana's band members were reportedly reluctant to appear on *MTV Unplugged* due to the show's format and uncertainty of how their music would be received in that type of setting.

After some hesitation and difficulties, Nirvana performed for 45 minutes on November 18, 1993, and the broadcast aired on December 16. Two songs, "Something in the Way" and "Oh Me," were cut. Though the band didn't play hits "Smells Like Teen Spirit" or "Lithium," their performance of "About a Girl," "Come As You Are," and other material made for a memorable musical event in rock 'n' roll history.

The album resulting from Nirvana's appearance, *MTV Unplugged in New York*, was released on November 1, 1994, debuting at number one and winning a Grammy for Best Alternative Music Album in 1996.

The album was released almost seven months after Kurt Cobain's suicide in April 1994 and consistently appears on many greatest-of-all-time lists. Their MTV performance was also released on DVD in 2007.

Nirvana's *Unplugged* performance is unique for several reasons, not the least of which includes their musical selections for the set, funereal stage decorations, use of guitar effects and electric amplification, and performances by Pat Smear, Lori Goldston, and Cris and Curt Kirkwood of the Meat Puppets. In addition, the band executed their 14-song performance in one take, with Cobain refusing an encore after ending the set with an emotional version of "Where Did You Sleep Last Night."

In retrospect, Nirvana's unique appearance on *MTV Unplugged* is intertwined with and magnified by the emotional loss of Kurt Cobain and the band's lost potential because of his death.

Nirvana's performance not only elevated the public's interest and love for *MTV Unplugged* as a series, but it shifted the balance of power and decision-making toward future bands and artists who appeared on the show.

Nirvana *Unplugged* epitomizes the ability of rock musicians to adapt their playing and interpretation of music, as well as the courage it takes to do so.

[68]
LANDMARK ALBUM: RADIOHEAD'S *OK COMPUTER*

Radiohead's landmark album, *OK Computer*, was released in 1997 as the English band's third studio album. This album was more experimental and unconventional than the group's previous work regarding its production—much of it was recorded live—and inclusion of techniques like natural reverberation and electronic instrumentation. *OK Computer* is visionary in its sound and narrative and epitomized the shift from pop to alternative rock among British bands.

Radiohead's *OK Computer* has been described as dystopian, with lyrics and music that paint a picture of fanatical capitalism and social alienation driven by digitization and consumerism. Its themes of overindulgence and dependence on technology inspire an overwhelming sense of the self-inflicted oppression created by modern life.

Though the album is a thoughtful and philosophical exploration of how political malice and technology threaten human culture, art, and individualism, many listeners find it less an expression of futility than an inspired call to action—socially and musically.

OK Computer solidified Radiohead's significance to alternative rock in terms of its music composition, but perhaps even more so for its social commentary and expression of modern isolation and alienation. Fans and critics agree that its themes and lyrics are just as relevant today, decades later.

The album reached number one in the UK and went double platinum in the US. Singles like "Paranoid Android," "Lucky," and "Karma Police" bolstered Radiohead's global presence and popularity. *OK Computer* won Best Alternative Music Album at the Grammys in 1998 and is considered one of the greatest and most influential albums of all time.

[69]
THE SEATTLE SOUND: SOUNDGARDEN AND ALICE IN CHAINS

In the early 1990s, Seattle became known for its "grunge" sound and bands—particularly Nirvana, Pearl Jam, Soundgarden, and Alice in Chains. Though the bands' members didn't always embrace the grunge label, their influence has extended far beyond the Pacific Northwest region and past the '90s.

First among many grunge acts to sign with Sub Pop, a record label based in Seattle, Soundgarden was formed in 1984 in Seattle by Chris Cornell (vocals, drums, rhythm guitar), Kim Thayil (lead guitar), and Hiro Yamamoto (bass). Cornell, Thayil, and Matt Cameron (drums) appear on each Soundgarden album, but the band's turnover was high. It was.

Soundgarden joined A&M Records in 1989, becoming the first grunge band to sign with a major label. In 1990, the album *Ultramega OK* was nominated for a Grammy, though commercial sales were low. Their third album, 1994's *Superunknown*, debuted at number one, with award-winning singles such as "Spoonman" and "Black Hole Sun."

Soundgarden disbanded in 1997, with members pursuing other projects, but formed again in 2010. However, when founding member Chris Cornell passed away in 2017, uncertainty regarding the future eventually led its members to retire the band's name, though they gathered in 2019 to perform at a tribute and fundraiser organized by Cornell's widow, Vicky.

Soundgarden is still considered a vital part of the Seattle grunge movement, as well as one of the greatest alternative/hard rock/heavy metal rock bands.

In 1987, Alice in Chains formed in Seattle and became associated with the grunge movement as well—though most consider their sound and style more resemblant to heavy metal. The band consistently featured two vocalists—Jerry Cantrell and Layne Staley—until Staley's death in 2002, at which point William DuVall joined the band. Other members include Sean Kinney (drums) and Mike Inez (bass), who replaced bassist Mike Starr after his death in 2011.

Alice in Chains gained early success with their albums *Facelift* in 1990, *Dirt* in 1992, and *Alice in Chains* in 1995. After a hiatus, the band re-formed in 2005 and released three albums from 2009-2018. Alice in Chains has received eleven Grammy nominations and is considered among the greatest hard rock groups.

[70]
BRITPOP BATTLE: OASIS VS. BLUR

The emergence of Britpop in the 1990s brought British alternative rock to the mainstream, particularly with the bands Blur and Oasis.

Oasis was founded in Manchester, England, in 1991. Despite the contentious professional relationship between original members and brothers Liam and Noel Gallagher, the group's debut album was a huge hit in the UK—followed by an even more successful second album, with hits such as "Wonderwall" and "Don't Look Back in Anger." Oasis won numerous awards in the mid-1990s, including British Album of the Year in 1996.

Blur, founded in London by Damon Albarn (lead singer), Graham Coxon (guitarist), Alex James (bassist), and Dave Rowntree (drummer), was established in 1988—a few years before Oasis. In 1994, Blur's "Girls & Boys" became their highest-charting single, and Blur won Best Band, Album, Single, and Video at the BRIT Awards in 1995. Though Blur has taken frequent breaks since the mid-2010s, the members have reunited occasionally to play, whereas Oasis disbanded in 2009.

Most Britpop fans would agree that the rivalry between Oasis and Blur began with Blur's sweep of the BRIT Awards in 1995. Both Gallagher brothers were vocal in their negativity about receiving just a single award and expressed their dislike of Blur in interviews. Unfortunately, the British press inflated the "battle" between the bands, portraying the situation as a clash between social classes rather than competition among musicians. Blur was painted in southern UK stereotypes as a band that came from a wealthier and more-educated background, whereas Oasis supposedly represented the northern UK working class. This led to the perception—by British audiences at least—of Blur as less genuine and authentic.

Overall, in terms of quantifiable sales, Oasis has outsold Blur in records by about eleven to one. However, Oasis's commercial success has more to do with the popularity of their single "Wonderwall" and a stronger presence in the US and international music scenes.

Hopefully, those who reflect on the brief Britpop battle between Oasis and Blur will recognize the negative influence of the press in exaggerating the animosity between both the bands and their fans through one-dimensional, stereotypical characterizations, and focus on the artists and their music instead.

PART EIGHT:
21ST-CENTURY ROCK

As the 1990s came to a close and the 21st century began, rock 'n' roll continued to diversify in its sounds and bands. Genres such as post-grunge, pop punk, and indie rock defined the early 2000s. In addition, the boundaries separating music, technology, consumerism, and global pop culture blurred further than ever, a phenomenon also reflected in 21st- century rock.

[71]
THE WHITE STRIPES: GARAGE ROCK REVIVAL

Jack White and Meg White formed the White Stripes in 1997 in Detroit, Michigan. This duo was significant in the garage rock revival and indie rock influence of the early 2000s, with Jack on guitar, keyboards, and vocals and Meg on drums and vocals. They found initial success within the Detroit music scene, and the release of their third album in 2001, *White Blood Cells*, brought them critical praise and commercial success, making them leaders of a garage rock revival.

The White Stripes went on to earn Grammys for their 2003 album *Elephant* and acclaim for their sixth and last album, *Icky Thump*, in 2007. The White Stripes disbanded in 2011.

The White Stripes merged garage rock with blues to achieve simplicity in their music and performance style. They were also rather sparing with public appearances, though well-known for their red, white, and black aesthetic.

Though the White Stripes only released six studio albums, their work is considered among the most definitive of all time due to their experimentation and pushing of genre restrictions. They were nominated for the Rock & Roll Hall of Fame in 2023 but were not inducted.

On February 2, 2011, Jack White and Meg White officially announced the breakup of the White Stripes, not due to any animosity but, reportedly, to keep the band's music legacy intact.

The White Stripes continue to influence artists in garage rock, blues, and even punk genres—especially in their unique performance style and sense of authenticity. Their songs "Icky Thump," "Seven Nation Army," and "Fell in Love with a Girl" remain popular among listeners and inspirational to current rock bands.

[72]
THE STROKES: NEW YORK'S COOLEST

The Strokes were a big part of the revival of post-punk and garage rock in the early 2000s. Forming in 1998 in New York City, members include singer/songwriter Julian Casablancas, guitarists Albert Hammond Jr. and Nick Valensi, and drummer Fabrizio Moretti. The Strokes' first album, *Is This It*, debuted to commercial and critical success in 2001.

Though the Strokes' first album didn't reach the US market until October of that year, many young Americans got ahold of and burned or copied the imported CD from Australia or the UK.

This method of acquiring and interacting with new music on CD not only introduced an organic yet tech-savvy way of sharing albums before high-speed internet, but it put the Strokes on the map with young audiences.

Subsequent albums in 2003 and 2006 didn't quite match the acclaim of their debut album, and the Strokes took a hiatus until 2011 with the release of *Angles*, then *Comedown Machine* in 2013. Casablancas founded his own label, Cult, and other members did primarily individual projects until 2020; at this point, the Strokes released *The New Abnormal*, winning a Grammy for Best Rock Album.

The Strokes' timing as a group, their music, and the early 21st-century rock culture allowed for even marginal alternative bands to become mainstream and commercial. The gritty, shabby-sounding music resulting from minimal studio production on albums like *Is This It* democratized the music industry, such that contemporary and future bands no longer felt the need to achieve a "perfect" sound. Rock' n' roll shifted to a DIY sound while retaining the benefits of record labels and other business support, so the process was not actually do-it-yourself.

The Strokes' individualism at the turn of the 21st century influenced groups such as the Killers, Arctic Monkeys, Kings of Leon, The National, and Vampire Weekend.

[73]
ARCTIC MONKEYS: INDIE ROCK SENSATION

The English rock band Arctic Monkeys formed in 2002 in Sheffield. Members include Alex Turner (vocals), Matt Helders (drums), Jamie Cook (guitar), and Nick O'Malley (bass.) In 2006, they released their first album, *Whatever People Say I Am, That's What I'm Not,* which led to commercial and critical success—making it the fastest-selling debut album in the UK. Arctic Monkeys' subsequent award-winning albums have also received critical acclaim, but their widespread international fame took root in 2013 with their album *AM* and hit song "Do I Wanna Know?"

Arctic Monkeys are considered among the first bands to utilize the internet and social media, such as Myspace, to gain a wide following and promote their music. The band embraced technology and boosted their popularity by handing out free demo CDs and expanding their internet fan base—an outlook that was ahead of most in the music industry. By sharing their music across social media, Arctic Monkeys pioneered a sense of connection and community among musicians and fans, allowing audiences a more organic approach to finding and appreciating independent artists.

Arctic Monkeys have won British Album of the Year and Best British Group three times, in addition to receiving nine Grammy nominations and making *Rolling Stone's* "500 Greatest Albums of All Time" list. Their individuality and relatable lyrics have set their music apart for over two decades, continuing to earn them young fans and influencing indie rock groups across the globe.

[74]
FOO FIGHTERS:
MODERN ROCK GIANTS

Dave Grohl, former drummer of Nirvana, founded Foo Fighters in Seattle in late 1994. Months after Kurt Cobain's death earlier that year, Grohl decided to focus on creating and recording solo material, which led to the Foo Fighters' self-titled debut album in 1995. Grohl played every instrument himself on the record, with one exception by guitarist Greg Dulli for "X-Static."

With the album's success, Grohl acquired bandmates, remaining lead singer and guitarist. For over a quarter of a century, with ten studio albums and hits such as "All My Life," "Everlong," and "Best of You," Foo Fighters have achieved critical acclaim and rock-star status among fans.

Originally, Foo Fighters comprised Dave Grohl, Pat Smear (guitar), Nate Mendel (bass), and William Goldsmith (drums.) Eventually, Chris Shifflet (guitar) and Taylor Hawkins (drums) joined Grohl and Mendel. Goldsmith did not return, though Smear rejoined in 2010, and keyboardist Rami Jaffe joined in 2016. Sadly, Hawkins died in March of 2022, and Josh Freese replaced him as drummer in 2023.

Foo Fighters' music has been characterized as alternative rock, post-grunge, hard rock, heavy punk rock, and even "dad" rock. Though their songs don't appear regularly on the Top 40 charts, the band enjoys a loyal fanbase that's both mainstream and diverse. Their concerts earn millions of dollars and are considered legendary by attendees of multiple generations— including dads.

Foo Fighters were inducted into the Rock & Roll Hall of Fame in 2021. This was Dave Grohl's second such honor, as he was initially inducted in 2014 as a member of Nirvana. The band has won 15 Grammys, setting a record for five Best Rock Album wins, and they were the first to receive the US Global Icon Award at the 2021 MTV Video Music Awards.

Foo Fighters are modern rock giants, blazing innovative paths for rock 'n' roll artists to reinvent themselves and their music while remaining true to fans and themselves. Grohl's incredible talent and vision as frontman, in addition to his nostalgic ties to Nirvana and approachable persona, are inarguably a large part of the Foo Fighters' appeal. However, the entire band has demonstrated their staying power and success through dedication, respect for their craft, and memorable music.

[75]
MUSE:
THEATRICAL AND BOMBASTIC

In 1994, Matt Bellamy (vocals, guitar), Chris Wolstenholme (vocals, bass), and Dominic Howard (drums) formed Muse in Devon, England. The band's roots began in the UK alternative rock scene, leading to a contract with Maverick Records and the release of their first album, *Showbiz*, in 1999. The album was considered melancholy but promising by several critics, who found it reminiscent of Radiohead's style. Muse's second album, *Origin of Symmetry*, received critical and commercial success in

2001 and is considered a landmark rock album in its instrumentation and ambitious concept influenced by the geometric structure of the universe.

Muse also developed a reputation for theatrical performances. Their stadium acts have often been compared to Queen, drawing large international audiences in the early 2000s.

Muse further showcased their eclectic blend of electronic, classical, art, and prog rock with their 2003 album, *Absolution*—another critical and commercial hit—including songs such as "Hysteria" and "Time Is Running Out."

Over the decades, Muse has continued to release albums exploring concepts of science fiction and themes of civil unrest and dystopia while giving bold arena rock performances around the world.

Muse has won two Grammys and eight NME awards, along with many other achievements in songwriting. Critics haven't always appreciated their quirky yet bombastic style, but the group has garnered a wide and dedicated fanbase. Their stadium shows, in particular, are known for being elaborate and making the group into mainstream rock stars, though some longtime fans believe that this has undermined their innovative sound and led to repetitive themes and more formulaic music.

Despite the peaks and valleys of Muse's career, they'll be remembered as an important part of 21st-century rock 'n' roll.

[76]
COLDPLAY:
ARENA ROCK SUPERSTARS

Coldplay formed in London in 1997, with members Chris Martin (vocals, piano), Jonny Buckland (guitar), Guy Berryman (bass), and Will Champion (drums.) Their contemporary alternative rock music is known the world over, as is their reputation for arena rock superstardom. In addition to being one of the bestselling rock groups of all time, Coldplay has significantly influenced 21st-century rock 'n' roll with iconic live performances, inclusivity, and advocacy.

Coldplay's members met at University College London and released their debut album, *Parachutes,* in 2000, with the hit song "Yellow." Since then, the British band has topped charts and received awards with subsequent albums and singles while incorporating different sounds and genres into their music, from R&B to gospel to progressive rock.

There's no doubt as to Coldplay's musical impact, yet their humanitarian and philanthropic activism have had a significant influence on popular culture as well. They're considered among the most environmentally-conscious touring musicians, making them leaders in climate activism around the world. In addition, Coldplay prioritizes accessibility for fans attending their concerts through sign language interpreters and sensory refuge stations, and it has reduced ticket prices through its Infinity Tickets program. Coldplay's global tours acknowledge the importance of representing indigenous cultures, and the group is also known for equality in their hiring practices.

Perhaps the biggest aspect of Coldplay's legacy is their reinvention of stadium performances and arena rock. The group has connected with fans in unprecedented ways, making them participants in their shows — as opposed to just audience members — through synced LED wristbands, covers of local songs, and guest performers.

Coldplay is also known for their sincerity, consistently conveyed by frontman Chris Martin and his personable interactions with stadium crowds, which make the experience surprisingly intimate for attendees despite the large crowds.

Coldplay will likely continue to revolutionize live performances in terms of sustainability, inclusivity, philanthropy, and commitment to excellence while remaining one of rock's most award-winning and commercially-successful groups of all time.

[77]
ICONIC PERFORMANCE: THE WHITE STRIPES' FINAL TOUR

In 2007, the White Stripes released *Icky Thump*, their sixth—and last—studio album, while touring at what appeared to be the height of their career. Playing multiple shows a day, Jack and Meg White traveled across the Atlantic and appeared on various television programs. Unfortunately, the intense tour escalated Meg's anxiety to such an extent that the band had to cancel their remaining performances.

The White Stripes' final performance took place on July 31, 2007, at the Snowden Grove Park Amphitheater in Southaven, Mississippi. This was to be their last show before a few weeks' break, after which the tour would resume. Meg White had been struggling, though, and the audience of 11,000 in Southaven just happened to catch their last tour performance. A few weeks later, in September, the White Stripes canceled the remainder of their 2007 tour, citing Meg's "acute anxiety."

In 2009, the White Stripes appeared on the final episode of *Late Night with Conan O'Brien* before officially disbanding in early 2011.

Today, musicians and bands seem to have a better awareness of the toll that touring can take on artists and, as a result, are more likely to cancel scheduled performances rather than risk their mental health or overall wellness. The White Stripes' final tour in 2007 brought this awareness to the forefront, encouraging understanding and support among fans.

[78]
LANDMARK ALBUM:
THE STROKES' *IS THIS IT*

In 2001, the Strokes released their debut album, *Is This It*. It had an immediate impact within the alternative rock genre, causing fans to label the group "saviors" of rock and launching Julian Casablancas to rock-star status as frontman. In the gap left by a waning grunge movement, the Strokes' sound was refreshing, serving as a counterbalance to other music at the time.

Part of the album's iconic nature results from the timing of its release in the US—two weeks after the September 11th attacks. Singles from the record include "Hard to Explain," "Last Nite," and "Someday," reflecting contemporary New York culture before the drastic change following 9/11.

In addition to the album's landmark music, its international cover art is iconic as well. It featured a Polaroid by photographer Colin Lane, a suggestive photo of a woman's hip with a hand on it in a leather glove. Though British retail chains objected to the cover, they stocked the album anyway. However, the Strokes changed the album cover for the American market to a psychedelic image of a bubble chamber with a subatomic particle.

Is This It has sold millions of copies across the world after making NME's Album of the Year in 2001. Critics still consider the Strokes' debut a landmark album, which influenced music across two decades. Bands such as the Killers, Arctic Monkeys, and Kings of Leon have credited it as inspiration, and artists such as Billie Eilish and Adele have expressed their admiration for the Strokes and their first album. *Is This It* has made its mark in the indie and alternative rock genres and will be remembered for reviving and reinventing garage rock in the 21st century.

[79]
THE RISE OF DIGITAL MUSIC: NAPSTER AND BEYOND

Technology has always influenced the music world, but perhaps never so much as the controversial rise of digital music. Digital music utilizes technology to record, create, convert, or distribute music. Compact discs (CDs) are an example of digital audio recording, as well as MP3s, which are compressed audio files. Digital formats make it easier to share music, and the advent of systems like Napster transformed not only the rock' n' roll industry but pop culture and the legal system as well.

Napster was created as a "peer-to-peer" platform for users to share and download digital music files for free. Founded by Shawn Fanning and Sean Parker, it became a sensation for millions of people, who could access an unprecedented amount of music at no cost. However, this also marked an extraordinary monetary disruption for the music business and a copyright and compensation nightmare for artists, leading to lawsuits brought by the Recording Industry Association of America and musicians including Metallica and Dr. Dre.

Napster was accused of facilitating copyright infringement, though they maintained that users were responsible for their own actions in sharing files. As a result, Napster was ordered to shut down in 2001, though the lawsuits raised questions regarding the protection of intellectual property in digital format while maintaining freedom of information and the internet marketplace.

The Napster controversy of the early 2000s resulted in legal platforms like iTunes and digital music streaming services such as Spotify, with ads or subscription fees allowing users to access music—and artists to be paid royalties for their work.

Though it can be tempting to lament the negative impacts of technology and digital music on rock 'n' roll, there have been—and continue to be—positive outcomes as well. With innovative digital technologies, musicians have access to more creative and less costly tools and sounds for composing, programming, and production. In addition, the rise of digital music platforms and streaming services has enabled greater access for the public to hear more diverse artists while increasing exposure for new musicians.

In many ways, digital music allows artists to have more direct interaction with fans and bypass the expense of big-business music distribution and publicity. These factors aren't without their problems but have democratized the rock 'n' roll industry and its artists—often providing greater opportunities for both creators and listeners.

[80]
ROCK IN THE AGE OF SOCIAL MEDIA: MYSPACE AND BANDCAMP

Next to the rise of digital music, social media will likely be considered the most critical element in the transformation and impact of 21st-century rock. From enabling "direct" interactions and communication between musicians and listeners to digital grass-roots marketing and promotion of diverse bands and artists, social media has offered unprecedented connections among rock 'n' roll fans and those who create it at a global level. Social media platforms facilitate live performances for audiences who may otherwise have limited access and allow fans to contribute to the music industry itself.

One of the most significant impacts social media has had on rock music is allowing for the discovery and widespread sharing of new and diverse music. Pioneering platforms like Myspace and Bandcamp promoted these activities at a global level.

From 2005 to 2008, Myspace became a popular social network for members to create profiles and share information, interests, and pictures. Bandcamp is an online music store that connects the community of fans with artists, providing opportunities to explore different music — most notably from artists outside the mainstream.

Since the new millennium, the proliferation of social media and rapid worldwide communication have exponentially increased the ability of fans to discover, share, and connect with musicians, their music, and other fans outside the limits of geography and radio play. In addition, social media gives artists — particularly independent and lesser-known groups — nearly unlimited access to performing and promoting their music to a global audience.

Though social media has posed certain problems for the rock music industry, such as copyright issues, privacy challenges, and a tremendous push for online content and presence, most people likely consider the impact a net positive. Listeners don't have to rely on traditional media sources to discover music, and musicians don't have to rely on record labels for marketing and promotion.

The unprecedented opportunities for exposure among fans and connection with diverse audiences are still growing. Ultimately, the age of social media allows for an expansive and cohesive sense of community for music lovers and rock 'n' roll creators.

PART NINE:
REGIONAL ROCK SCENES

Across the US, certain regions have become deeply associated with rock 'n' roll movements and performers. Though it's difficult to predict which area will become known for a certain kind of music — and even tougher to pinpoint why, when, and where — it's clear that regional rock scenes have birthed new genres, music forms, and inspirational artists. In many ways, these are time capsules of the era, people, and culture coming together through musical expression, reflecting the impact of local sounds and diverse fans and creating a unique relationship among art, time, and space.

[81]
SAN FRANCISCO: THE SUMMER OF LOVE

The Summer of Love brought thousands of people to San Francisco, mingling the sentiments of free love and spirituality with psychedelia, Vietnam War opposition, and other aspects of "hippie" culture. Hippies and "flower children" were general, if pejorative, terms used to describe a diverse group of people sharing anti-government, anti-consumer, anti-suburbia, and anti-war sentiments. Though many were active participants in political protests, most took part in counterculture art and music, as well as nontraditional spiritual practices and hallucinogens.

Perhaps nothing epitomizes the Summer of Love and resulting San Francisco sound than John Phillips's "San Francisco (Be Sure to Wear Flowers in Your Hair)," released by the Mamas & the Papas in May 1967. Other groups to come out of the Bay Area include Santana, Creedence Clearwater Revival (CCR), Jefferson Airplane, the Grateful Dead, and Journey.

From its jazz and blues roots of the 1950s to the psychedelic rock of the 1960s, the music of San Francisco has always represented innovation. This has carried through to experimentation with lyrics and music in the punk genre and indie rock movements as well.

The San Francisco rock scene, symbolized by 1967's Summer of Love, inspired legendary musicians—and continues to do so, representing a decade of social revolution and counterculture. Nostalgia for the era has made its mark on subsequent generations, as shown in movies, television, and even Broadway revivals of the late-1960s rock musical *Hair*.

[82]
DETROIT:
THE MOTOR CITY SOUND

Detroit has had a significant impact on rock 'n' roll, beginning with roots in blues and jazz. In 1956, inspired by the music of Bill Haley—who was from a Detroit suburb—and Elvis Presley, *Detroit Teen Life* became the first teen-oriented newspaper with features important to youth culture. Combined with the Motor City's car industry, especially in the '60s and '70s, Detroit's ties to innovative music and rock-star imagery remain strong to this day.

Perhaps the most important influence on the Motor City's sound was Berry Gordy Jr., who founded Motown Record Corporation in 1960. Motown produced some of the greatest singer-songwriters, bands, and songs in the history of American music. Among the numerous legendary Motown artists are Marvin Gaye, Diana Ross, Smokey Robinson, the Temptations, Stevie Wonder, and The Jackson 5. Gordy's tremendous success and contribution to the world of music are attributed in part to his emphasis on the quality and support of Black artists.

At the other end of the spectrum lies the rise of garage rock bands in the 1960s, including the Stooges and their frontman, Iggy Pop. Iggy Pop loomed large in the Detroit underground rock scene and heavily influenced punk music.

Alice Cooper, also from Detroit, integrated Motor City sound into his music—a mix of R&B, Motown, and guitar rock. Overall, the Detroit rock scene is based on diversity, and its legacy continues to inspire rock music and musicians today.

[83]
SEATTLE:
GRUNGE CAPITAL

Grunge music has been closely associated with Seattle, Washington, since the mainstream success of Nirvana's *Nevermind* in 1991. That year also saw the release of *Ten* by Pearl Jam and Soundgarden's *Badmotorfinger*, followed by *Dirt* by Alice in Chains the next year.

These Seattle bands were put in the grunge category, though some consider this more of a catch-all regional label than the definition of a particular sound or music genre. However, the commercial popularity and success of Seattle's grunge records and musicians spread throughout the globe in the 1990s, inspiring other alternative, non-Seattle rock groups with an "unpolished" sound, such as Stone Temple Pilots.

Though the term "grunge" was actually used to characterize certain bands as long ago as the 1960s, it was first applied to Seattle's music scene in 1987 by Bruce Pavitt in reference to Green River's album *Dry as a Bone*. As up-and-coming northwestern bands faced low-budget, somewhat-amateur recording and production circumstances, their "dirty" sound became intimately associated with Seattle and music that seemed less commercial and industry-manufactured in its appeal.

Many rock historians cite certain features of Seattle and the surrounding cities that made it the grunge capital of the 1990s, such as its geographical and cultural isolation from other major cities, the working-class economic realities of the region, and the antiestablishment, nonconformist values of young artists and audiences in the Pacific Northwest.

Sub Pop, an independent record label in Seattle, capitalized on the growing underground movement, combining punk and metal by marketing music and performers as "grunge." Ultimately, this associated the term grunge with the subculture originating in Seattle in the late 1980s and early 1990s, as well as a type of alternative rock music that defined a decade.

[84]
MANCHESTER: THE BIRTHPLACE OF BRITPOP

Manchester, England, has long been associated with rock 'n' roll, from the Hollies in the 1960s to the Smiths and New Order in the 1980s. In the 1990s, Manchester became the birthplace of Britpop with independent bands like Oasis, Blur, and Suede. Overall, Britpop features guitar music with catchy melodies and introspective lyrical references to UK culture and identity — especially those of the working class.

Though the genre seemed to be a reaction against the 1990s American grunge music scene, many Britpop bands were influenced by and paid homage to classic British groups like the Beatles, the Rolling Stones, and the Kinks.

Britpop spread from Manchester to become a global phenomenon, notably due to the inflated publicity of Oasis and Blur's rivalry. The lyrics of Britpop songs were particularly relevant to British youth, inspiring a cultural movement of UK pride that came to be known as "Cool Britannia."

Though Britpop's popularity waned around the beginning of the 21st century, ultimately, the Manchester British bands of the 1990s helped define a musical decade and genre that celebrated the working-class identity of those in the UK and revived the roots of classic British rock.

[85]
NEW YORK:
PUNK ROCK CENTRAL

From the early 1970s to the mid-1990s, New York City was the central scene for punk rock. Clubs and venues such as Max's Kansas City and St. Mark's Place saw a thriving and appreciative audience for what would become legendary punk bands. Yet there was no more iconic club for underground performances and punk rock culture than NYC's CBGB.

CBGB was founded in 1973 by Hilly Kristal in the Bowery area of Lower Manhattan. This club quickly became the center of NYC's punk scene, hosting bands such as the Ramones, Talking Heads, Blondie, the Patti Smith Group, and Joan Jett. The full name of the venue was CBGB & OMFUG, which is short for Country, Bluegrass, Blues, and Other Music for Uplifting Gormandizers — music forms that the club initially intended to feature. However, by 1974, CBGB was a hub for rock, American punk, and new wave bands, all part of NYC's underground punk rock scene.

Over two decades, CBGB became home to hardcore punk, metal, and alternative rock groups such as Agnostic Front, Youth of Today, Korn, Green Day, and Guns N' Roses. CBGB closed in 2006, with Patti Smith as its final performer. In 2012, the CBGB Festival became the largest in NYC, hosting free concerts in Times Square and Central Park. A year later, CBGB was added to the National Register of Historic Places, and it continues to be a frequent site for visiting music fans of all types.

New York City continues to embrace and celebrate punk rock with themed exhibits at the Metropolitan Museum of Art, the Museum of Modern Art, and the Museum of Arts and Design, in addition to landmarks like CBGB.

The punk scene of the 1970s launched a new genre of American music and culture, paving the way for further evolutions of rock 'n' roll and its importance to New York and beyond.

[86]
LOS ANGELES: HAIR METAL HEAVEN

Many people associate Los Angeles with Hollywood and movies, but it's also an important location for regional rock 'n' roll. Several recording studios, including Capitol Records, are located in LA. In the 1960s, venues and clubs along Sunset Boulevard, the "Sunset Strip," featured bands like the Byrds and the Doors, and music from the Beach Boys came to symbolize California sound. The punk rock movement of the early to mid-1970s also had a significant presence in Los Angeles.

By the late 1970s and into the 1980s, LA became a hair metal heaven with the West Coast heavy metal movement. Famous clubs along the Sunset Strip, including Whisky a Go Go and the Roxy, hosted metal bands such as Van Halen, Mötley Crüe, Quiet Riot, and Guns N' Roses. This inspired hair and glam metal fashion trends as much as a rock music movement. The LA music scene also paved the way for thrash metal bands like Metallica, Megadeth, and Slayer, in addition to alternative and metal bands like Red Hot Chili Peppers, Jane's Addiction, and Rage Against the Machine.

Los Angeles remains a vibrant area of opportunity and creative expression for rock 'n' roll artists.

[87]
LONDON:
THE HEART OF BRITISH ROCK

London has been the heart of British rock music since the early 1960s, and its contribution to the world of rock 'n' roll continues to grow. From the unprecedented impact of the Beatles and the Rolling Stones to Pink Floyd, the Who, The Clash, and the Sex Pistols, London has produced legendary artists spanning decades. Though rock' n' roll may have initially traveled from the US to the UK, London soon became a global source of unique talent and innovative music blends and genres — leading to more than one "British invasion."

London is a city of diverse cultures, classes, and ideologies, allowing for collaboration among musicians and artists. In addition, the British art-school system has significantly influenced many London rock band members, not only as an escape from traditional and urban life but as a path for experimentation and innovation. From Abbey Road to the 100 Club, London remains an integral, influential, and important regional rock scene.

[88]
AUSTIN:
LIVE MUSIC CAPITAL OF THE WORLD

Not only is Austin the state capital of Texas, but the city's official motto has been the "Live Music Capital of the World" since 1991. Austin features numerous live music venues concentrated in districts throughout the city and is internationally recognized for festivals such as South by Southwest (SXSW) and Austin City Limits (ACL). The slogan has encouraged tourism from around

120

the world in addition to artists across the rock' n' roll spectrum, including punk, new wave, alternative, and indie bands.

Austin became an important counterculture music region in the early 1970s, with the opening of Armadillo World Headquarters—a venue that hosted both country and rock music shows. For decades, the city has attracted innovative artists with its support of creativity, inclusion, and year-round performance opportunities.

The live music industry in Austin is valued at nearly $2 billion, primarily due to the widespread popularity of SXSW and ACL, in addition to over 30 other annual music festivals. ACL alone has hosted several rock legends across many generations, including Jerry Lee Lewis, Florence and the Machine, Billie Eilish, Coldplay, Dave Matthews Band, St. Vincent, the Strokes, Jewel, the Killers, John Mayer, Muse, Nine Inch Nails, Foo Fighters, Arctic Monkeys, and the Allman Brothers Band. Other bands associated with Austin include Asleep at the Wheel, Spoon, Double Trouble, The Mrs, the Impossibles, Harlem, and Goudie.

Though the "live music capital of the world" is more or less Austin's "brand" when it comes to tourism and entertainment, there are multiple reasons to substantiate this claim. More than 250 music venues exist in the city, reportedly hosting concerts each night of the year—adding up to thousands of live shows and performances annually. In addition, the variety of quality venues makes concertgoing a positive experience for music enthusiasts, both native to Austin and around the globe.

[89]
NASHVILLE:
MORE THAN COUNTRY

Most people associate country music with Nashville, Tennessee, as it's home to the Grand Ole Opry and Country Music Hall of Fame. However, the diversity of musical history within the region, represented in the Music Hall of Fame and other sites, goes beyond the country genre — truly making it America's "Music City." Today, Nashville offers live music and clubs that run the spectrum of rock 'n' roll, including punk, metal, alternative, and indie.

Rock music has been integral to Nashville since the mid-1950s. RCA Studio B was particularly important to the rock 'n' roll aspect of Nashville's sound and a foundational international recording center that's now part of the city's Music Row. Elvis Presley signed with RCA in 1955 and ended up recording over 240 songs in Studio B. Roy Orbison, and the Everly Brothers recorded there, as well.

Nashville's vibrant music scene has allowed many artists to establish themselves as performers and provided opportunities for studio recordings. In the early 1960s, Jimi Hendrix began his professional career performing in downtown clubs. Other well-known rock bands and musicians associated with Nashville across the decades include Little Richard, Bob Dylan, Peter Frampton, Noah Cyrus, the Pink Spiders, the Semantics, Jack White, Paramore, and Taylor Swift.

Nashville continues to prove that its music scene offers more than just country, with various rock clubs that support and feature local talent as well as internationally famous bands. Venues such as Exit/In, The 5 Spot, and the Basement offer live performances of up-and-coming and established artists while promoting collaboration and inclusivity. These clubs have hosted legendary musicians, including the Red Hot Chili Peppers, R.E.M., the Lumineers, Maren Morris, Linda Ronstadt, and Metallica.

Though Nashville will remain strong in its country roots, it will no doubt maintain its historical reputation as a regional rock scene as well.

[90]
THE SOUTHERN ROCK SCENE: LYNYRD SKYNYRD AND THE ALLMAN BROTHERS

Southern rock is not only a subgenre of rock 'n' roll but a regional music scene of the American South, distinguished by a mix of rock, country, and blues in addition to lyrics that reflect the unique culture of life in southern America. Iconic instrumentation, guitar solos, and lyrical storytelling define the region's sound, history, and evolving culture.

In the 1970s, bands such as Lynyrd Skynyrd, the Allman Brothers Band, and the Ozark Mountain Daredevils popularized southern rock and brought the region's musical style to America's mainstream and a global audience, as well. Iconic songs such as "Sweet Home Alabama," "Free Bird" (Lynyrd Skynyrd), and "Ramblin' Man" (Allman Brothers) became generational anthems, blending rock with the sound of southern blues and narrative lyrics. As musical styles evolved toward the end of the 20th century, groups such as 38 Special, ZZ Top, Molly Hatchet, the Black Crowes, Tom Petty and the Heartbreakers, and Corrosion of Conformity have continued to achieve success while maintaining their Southern rock roots.

The southern rock scene encompasses a wide area of the US and embraces a wide variety of musical influences, including country, heavy metal, blues, hard rock, and even jazz. Legendary southern rock artists Lynyrd Skynyrd and the Allman Brothers are among the pioneers of this rock 'n' roll genre, which encapsulates the traditions, pride, spirit, and musical history of the American South. However, new bands and musicians continue the Southern rock legacy while adding contemporary perspectives and innovative sound.

PART TEN:
ICONIC ROCK FESTIVALS

Besides various landmark and memorable performances by individual bands, rock 'n' roll is also known for iconic festivals that brought legendary musicians and diverse audiences together for a shared experience beyond a traditional concert performance. Rock festivals have not only provided a platform for different music and performers but have also inspired social awareness and action, promoted individuality and inclusivity and demonstrated the impact of rock 'n' roll on communities, culture, and history.

Of course, some people may have a more cynical attitude toward rock festivals — especially today — in terms of their commercial business ventures, manufactured lineups, and negative environmental impacts. Yet it's undeniable that music festivals offer unique opportunities for artistic expression and appreciation, cultural exchanges, and a sense of inclusion in potentially important and historic events.

[91]
WOODSTOCK 1969: PEACE AND MUSIC

Perhaps the most iconic and famous rock festival took place in August 1969: the Woodstock Music and Art Fair. Over 500,000 people came to a 600-acre dairy farm in Bethel, New York, to hear new and established performers play from August 15-18. Among the festival's 32 acts were the Who, Jimi Hendrix, Janis Joplin, the Grateful Dead, Joan Baez, Carlos Santana, and CCR.

The four producers of the Woodstock festival were Artie Kornfield, Michael Lang, John Robers, and Joel Rosenman. Not only did they woefully underestimate the number of attendees, but they did not take bad weather, food and water shortages, and inadequate sanitation into consideration. Despite the circumstances — and turnout of half a million people — Woodstock lived up to its message of unity and peace and incredible music.

Woodstock '69 is considered one of the greatest cultural and memorable musical events in history. The connection between the audience and performers expanded across the country and globe, resulting in a pivotal moment for the counterculture movements of the 1960s and demonstrating the power of music in generating a collective purpose.

Not only did Woodstock bring diverse musical acts together, but it also reflected the way rock' n' roll could reach an entire generation. Amid the political havoc and social protests of 1969, including the Vietnam War, the civil rights movement, and the rise of the hippy subculture, Woodstock represented freedom, diversity, and the hope of many young people that change was indeed possible.

[92]
ISLE OF WIGHT FESTIVAL: BRITISH WOODSTOCK

The Isle of Wight Festival of 1970 is regarded as the European counterpart to America's Woodstock. Over 600,000 people attended the five-day counterculture music festival on an island off the southern coast of England, enjoying legendary artists such as the Who, the Doors, Leonard Cohen, Jimi Hendrix, Joni Mitchell, and Joan Baez.

Though the festival was held in 1968 and 1969, in 1970, it attracted unprecedented crowds, leading to security concerns and an overwhelmed local population. Local authorities prohibited the festival for 30 years because of what they viewed as a threat to safety and an organizational nightmare.

Since its return in 2002, produced and curated by John Giddings, the festival has hosted musicians such as the Rolling Stones, The Police, Blondie, the Sex Pistols, Pearl Jam, Paul McCartney, Coldplay, Foo Fighters, David Bowie, and Bruce Springsteen.

For the past two decades, staff and promoters of the festival have focused on safety, sustainability, and community relations for attendees and performers. The festival has also recently embraced hip-hop acts and avant-garde jazz musicians, in addition to family-friendly performances.

[93]
LIVE AID 1985:
ROCK FOR A CAUSE

Live Aid took place on July 13, 1985, a global fundraising initiative culminating in a benefit concert held in two venues at the same time: Wembley Stadium in London and John F. Kennedy Stadium in Philadelphia.

The event's organizers, Bob Geldof, and Midge Ure, were raising funds to end the brutal famine taking place in Ethiopia and other areas on the African continent at the time. Live Aid was viewed in 150 countries, with an estimated audience between 1.5 and 2 billion people, making it one of the largest satellite broadcasts in the history of television.

There were some positive results from Live Aid: It raised over $140 million for famine relief and put a global spotlight on the food shortages in African nations.

The humanitarian intentions of the organizers, musical acts, and others involved were legitimate — especially in representing music as a vehicle for uniting people worldwide to support a greater cause. In addition, the 16-hour event featured performances from over 75 of the most legendary rock 'n' roll musicians of the 1980s, including Elton John, U2, David Bowie, Madonna, Tina Turner, Paul McCartney, and Queen.

Unfortunately, many people at the time — even more since — have recognized that the issues of famine in Africa had been portrayed in a simplistic, patronizing manner. The subtext of the campaign to fix complex problems by handing over large sums of money revealed a level of "White saviorism" that seems shocking and almost cartoonish 40 years later.

[94]
GLASTONBURY FESTIVAL: UK'S PREMIER FESTIVAL

The Glastonbury Festival takes place in England during the summer and is considered the UK's premier performing arts festival and a part of British culture. It lasts for five days and includes music, along with comedy, dance, theater, and more. Unlike other music and arts festivals, the Glastonbury Festival is not held annually, allowing for "fallow" years to give the area and community time to recover. Michael Eavis hosted the first Glastonbury Festival in the fall of 1970, inspired by the counterculture movements of the 1960s.

Many legendary pop and rock musicians have headlined "Glasto," drawing thousands of fans on acres of farmland. In 1971, the festival introduced the "Pyramid Stage," a replica of the Great Pyramid of Giza, which has been rebuilt several times over the years. The Pyramid Stage has hosted many iconic performances from artists including Radiohead, Coldplay, Muse, Oasis, Blur, Bruce Springsteen, Neil Young, Beyoncé, Elton John, Arctic Monkeys, Foo Fighters, Guns N' Roses, Billie Eilish, and Florence and the Machine.

Volunteers largely run the Glastonbury Festival, and most of the festival profits are donated to charity.

In its five decades of existence, the Glastonbury Festival has endured intense heat, storms, flooding, overcrowding, security fence breaches, fighting, and crime. In addition, the debris and waste left behind by attendees have created a negative impact on the environment, leading festival staff to adopt greener efforts, including free, biodegradable tent pegs and other environmentally-friendly initiatives.

[95]
COACHELLA: THE MODERN ROCK FESTIVAL

The first Coachella music festival took place in October 1999, featuring alternative rock musicians such as Rage Against the Machine, Morrissey, and Beck. Now held annually in the Coachella Valley of Indio, California, Coachella is considered a cultural touchstone known for its celebrity influence and social media presence, as well as its diverse music.

Paul Tollet, founder of Goldenvoice, organized the first Coachella festival as a singular event. Due to its popularity, the festival became an annual counterculture gathering, attracting alternative rock and indie bands, celebrity and fashion icons, and featuring interactive art installations.

The Coachella festival expanded in the new millennium, adding hip-hop, pop, and other acts to the roster, as well as headliners such as Radiohead, Paul McCartney, Prince, and Beyoncé.

The festival is known for supporting diverse music genres, including electronic dance music. Bands like the Killers and Arctic Monkeys gained newfound success after performing at Coachella. However, the festival has been criticized for its lack of representation of women, BIPOC, and LGBTQIA+ artists and headliners.

The incorporation of technology is among the biggest impacts Coachella has made on music and overall culture. This includes everything from interactive and augmented reality art installations to extended exposure on social media platforms.

Coachella is committed to expansion, inclusivity, and innovation each year, providing fans with new music, launching new artistic

130

talent, and having an enormous impact on the evolution of popular and modern festival culture.

[96]
READING AND LEEDS FESTIVALS: ROCK' N' ROLL STAPLES

Two staples of rock 'n' roll music festivals in England are the Reading and Leeds Festivals, both taking place annually in August.

The Reading Festival, originally the National Jazz Festival, is held at Little John's Farm in Reading. It's the oldest pop music festival in the UK and was first held in 1971.

In 1999, the first Leeds Festival took place in Bramham Park, near Wetherby, on the grounds of a historic house. The venues are 200 miles apart, allowing visitors to camp at either site or buy day tickets to each—or both. In most cases, the musical acts play both festivals on different days, with lineups that include rock, indie, punk, metal, alternative, and even hip-hop artists.

Reading and Leeds have hosted legendary bands from Britain and other nations, including the Beastie Boys, Rage Against the Machine, Nirvana, Black Sabbath, Public Enemy, the Cure, Muse, Hole, Kendrick Lamar, Metallica, Dua Lipa, and Billie Eilish. In recent years, both festival sites have expanded to accommodate larger crowds.

As with many festivals, though the Reading and Leeds Festivals continue to diversify and grow in popularity, they present safety concerns. In addition, there's an unfortunate tradition of "bottling," in which bottles are thrown at certain acts to force them offstage. However, festival organizers continue to improve safety measures.

PART ELEVEN: ROCK 'N' ROLL TRIVIA AND FUN FACTS

There's no shortage of trivia and fun facts when it comes to the world of rock 'n' roll, from the actual given names of rock stars to alleged band antics, all of which add up to a fascinating portrait of the genre. Though it's difficult to separate fact from fiction among the urban legends of rock 'n' roll, here are a few interesting bits of information to consider.

[97]
THE ORIGINS OF THE TERM "ROCK 'N' ROLL"

There's no way to directly trace to the origin of the term "rock 'n' roll," but musicologists agree on some historical and cultural factors that established the term in our modern lexicon. From the 17th century, sailors would use the phrase "rocking and rolling" to describe a ship's motion, and this phrase became a metaphor—and sometimes euphemism—for dancing or sex in the 1920s. In 1922, a blues song by Trixie Smith was titled "My Man Rocks Me (With One Steady Roll)," which appears to be the first mention of the phrase in a musical context.

Ultimately, it was Alan Freed who popularized the term "rock 'n' roll" in the early 1950s. Freed was a DJ in Cleveland, Ohio, at the time. He called his show "The Rock and Roll Session" to categorize the mixture of R&B and country music that he played. Freed's radio show reached mainstream America, as did the music, and the term rock 'n' roll was born.

[98]
THE MOST COVERED ROCK SONG

A "cover" is a reinterpretation of an original song. Various artists have covered many classic rock songs; however, according to the

Guinness Book of Records, the song "Yesterday" by the Beatles is the most-covered song in history.

Though many listeners may consider "Yesterday" more of a ballad, the Beatles originally recorded it as a pop rock song in 1965 for their album *Help!* There have been over 3,000 recorded cover versions of "Yesterday" and an estimated seven million performances of the song as of 2001.

Various artists who have covered "Yesterday" include Frank Sinatra, Joan Baez, Liberace, Ray Charles, Boyz II Men, Aretha Franklin, Maroon 5, Neil Diamond, and Elvis Presley. In 2006, Paul McCartney performed "Yesterday" along with Linkin Park and Jay-Z's "Numb/Encore" at the Grammy Awards.

[99]
THE LONGEST
ROCK SONG

In the '70s, there was a movement in rock 'n' roll toward long-form music among many bands and singer-songwriters. This trend may have been due, in part, to musical experimentation or perhaps a rebellion against the traditional three-minute pop single format typical of radio play in the 1950s and 1960s. Many of the longer rock songs of the '70s onward are associated with progressive or "prog" rock—a subgenre influenced by classical music, keyboard, and lengthy instrumentation and composition.

Some of the longest rock songs include "2112" by Rush, "Shine on You Crazy Diamond" by Pink Floyd, and "Mountain Jam" by the Allman Brothers Band. However, most agree that progressive rock band Jethro Tull's "Thick as a Brick" is the longest popular rock song to be recorded. The song is the only track on the album of the same name, running nearly 44 minutes. In 1972, the song was shortened so a sample could be played on the radio.

[100]
THE MOST EXPENSIVE
ROCK ALBUM

In the 1960s, some of the most groundbreaking and well-known rock albums came at record-breaking costs, including *Sgt. Pepper's Lonely Hearts Club Band* (1967, the Beatles), *Tommy* (1969, the Who), and *Pet Sounds* (1966, the Beach Boys.) In 1979, Fleetwood Mac's *Tusk* was the first album to cost more than $1 million to produce. *Chinese Democracy* by Guns N' Roses holds the Guinness World Record for the most expensive album at about $13 million.

However, Michael Jackson's final album, *Invincible,* released in 2001, topped them all, costing between $30 million and $40 million to produce. *Invincible*, a multi-genre mix of R&B, soul, and pop, not only features Michael Jackson but over 100 other musicians, such as Kanye West, the Notorious B.I.G., Slash, and Carlos Santana.

[101]
THE FUTURE OF ROCK 'N' ROLL:
EMERGING BANDS AND TRENDS

It's difficult to predict the future of rock 'n' roll or what bands and trends will emerge. Technology, artistic creativity, and decades of musical history will continue to influence musicians, styles, and sounds, along with pop culture, movies, video games, and social and political ideology. Future singer-songwriters and musicians are also likely to take up rock's legacy of challenging traditions and pushing boundaries, reinventing and honoring this important music genre.

CONCLUSION:

THE ENDURING SPIRIT OF ROCK 'N' ROLL

From its beginnings, rock 'n' roll has been associated with freedom and youth culture, crossing geographic, cultural, and racial boundaries to provide a voice for rebellion, protest, and change. For generations, rock music has proved a cultural touchstone and a means of personal connection across the globe. Whether the genre is classic rock, heavy metal, punk, alternative, or otherwise, the spirit of rock 'n' roll is based on innovative sound, musical artistry, and lyrics that resonate with a vast and diverse audience.

Rock music not only reflects the history, culture, and art of its time but also that which is transformative and revolutionary. The influence of rock pioneers and legends will continue to inspire listeners and creators, connecting people across time, place, and cultures and allowing new voices, styles, and sounds to take root. Ultimately, these factors ensure that the spirit of rock 'n' roll will not only evolve but endure for generations to come.